possibilities

365 Daily Devotions

MATTHEW KELLY

BLUE SPARROW BOOKS

North Palm Beach, Florida

blue sparrow

Copyright © 2020
Kakadu, LLC
Published by BLUE SPARROW BOOKS

Design by Ashley Wirfel

ISBN: 978-1-63582-163-5 (hardcover)
ISBN: 978-1-63582-162-8 (e-Book)

10   9   8   7   6   5   4   3   2   1

Printed in the United States of America

FIRST EDITION

table of contents

*The measure of your life will be
the measure of your courage.*

introduction

WE LIVE IN a world of unlimited possibilities, but too often we get caught up in the day-to-day realities of life and the hustle and bustle of the world and lose sight of all that is possible.

The busier our lives become, the more important it is to live with great intentionality. The more options we have before us, the more important it is to discern and decide with great intentionality.

And living with great intentionality requires that we step back from time to time and think about life. We live more fulfilling lives when we pause each day to think about who we are, what we are here for, what matters most, what matters least, and our hopes and dreams for tomorrow.

Who are you?

What are you here on this earth at this time for?

What matters most to you?

What matters least to you?

Do the ways you spend your time, energy, money, and attention reflect what matters most to you?

What are your hopes for today?

What are your dreams for tomorrow?

It is my great hope that as we make this journey together over the next year, the answers to these questions will begin to unfold in your heart. As they do I believe you will be given astounding clarity about your life as it is today and your life as in can be in the future.

Little by little chaos and confusion will give way to clarity and courage. With that piercing clarity you will begin to see all the amazing possibilities that exist within you and around you. And that clarity will fill you with the courage you need to embrace, chase, accept, or surrender to all the amazing possibilities that are waiting for you.

MATTHEW KELLY

january

January 1

WHEN I WAS twelve years old, I used to sing in the school choir, and often we would sing at funerals. Whether or not I knew the person who had died, funerals have always had a deep impact on my life. Every time I go to a funeral, or hear that someone I know has died, I always become more determined not to waste my life, not to take life for granted.

Every now and then I like to take a walk in a cemetery. Each tombstone tells a story. Some of the people were laid to rest last year, others a hundred years ago. Some of them lived for ninety-five years, others for twenty-five years. But I can hear all of them calling out to me in unison, sharing with me a message: "Life is short. Do not waste your life. Live life passionately."

january 2

YOUR DAILY TASKS have spiritual value. You don't
work just for money. When you work hard and pay attention to the details of your job, you cooperate with God as
he transforms your soul. In this way your work helps you
to become more fully yourself. It is also a way to love your
neighbor and make a contribution to society. In the same
way, washing the dishes can be as much a prayer as praying the rosary. Each task, each hour offered to God is transformed into prayer. And in all these ways you give glory to
God through your daily work.

january 3

GOD'S DREAMS for you and me go far beyond what the world has to offer. He made each and every single one of us wonderfully unique, and he dreams that we will chase, embrace and celebrate all he created us to be: the-very-best-version-of-ourselves. Though we take pride in our individualism and independence we seem particularly enamored of fitting in. To a certain extent, the desire to fit in and be accepted is natural and normal. But when it comes at the cost of losing sight of who we are as marvelously unique individuals, something is amiss. Let us seek to discover once more what it means to be perfectly ourselves.

january 4

_____

DO YOU KNOW what you want?

Most people can tell you exactly what they don't want, but very few have the same clarity about what they do want.

If you don't know what you want from life, everything will appear either as an obstacle or as a burden. But one of the great lessons of history is that the whole world gets out of the way for people who know what they want or where they are going. Be assured, if you don't know where you are going, you are lost.

Do not say, "I am too old."

Don't say, "I'm too young."

Tiger Woods was three years old when he shot 48 for nine holes on his hometown golf course in Cypress, California . . . Michelangelo was seventy-two years old when he designed the dome of St. Peter's Basilica in Rome . . . Whether you are sixteen or sixty, the rest of your life is ahead of you. You cannot change one moment of your past, but you can change your whole future. Now is your time.

january 5

_____

DO NOT BE AFRAID of possibilities. There are always so many more than the ones you see easily. Take time to reflect. Look deeper. Seek out the unseen opportunities that you have overlooked at first glance. Possibilities abound. You and I—human beings—are capable of incredible things . . . We underestimate ourselves, but God never does. He knows exactly what you are capable of in collaboration with him. Allow God to raise up the saint in you. This is what your corner of the world needs right now.

january 6

_____

DREAMS ARE invisible, but powerful. Think for a moment of electricity. You cannot see it, but it keeps everything going. Invisible, but powerful! If, for a moment, you doubt the power of electricity, consider what would happen if you stuck your finger into an electrical outlet. You would quickly be reminded of its power. Should you doubt that electricity keeps everything going, may I suggest that you turn off the electricity at your office tomorrow! I think you will find that little if anything gets done and that most of your employees will go home for the day.

So it is with dreams. They are invisible, but powerful. You cannot see them, but they keep everything going.

january 7

THERE IS ONE question that I want to ask you as we begin this journey together: Do you believe it is possible to be happier than you have been at any other time in your life? Think about that. Don't just read on. Pause for a moment and reflect. Do you believe it is possible to be happier than you have ever been?

Real happiness is a sign that the human spirit is thriving. This is the thriving I yearn for and the thriving I suspect you are hungry for. We want to live life more fully; we're impatient to live life to the fullest. So wherever your happiness project is right now, even if it is a complete train wreck, all I am asking you to do right now is open yourself to the possibility that God wants you to experience a happiness greater than you have ever experienced before in your life. Stay open.

january 8

_____

IT IS TOO EASY to let another week, month, year slip by without really thinking about the life we want to live. It is too easy to just let life happen to us. We don't sit down often enough and think about how we are living. We continue to spend more time planning our annual vacations than we spend planning our lives. This has to change if we are to enjoy immense satisfaction personally and professionally. You can stumble into a moderately satisfying life, but to sustain and increase that satisfaction requires a strategic approach and some real work. The promise of this book is that you can be the architect of a life that is both personally and professionally satisfying. But in order to design and build such a life for yourself, you will need to approach this task with the rigor and commitment the best companies in the world use to approach the development of a new product. There are many different ways you could live your life. Your talents, personality, and relationships make many lives possible. There are many paths you can choose to follow both personally and professionally. You don't have to settle for the life you stumbled into.

january 9

_____

PEACE IS NOT the absence of pain or pressure. Nor is it the absence of activity. Peace is not lying on a beach without a worry in the world. Peace is not born by doing nothing.

This peace I speak of is a certainty in my heart and mind that I am using my life for a worthy purpose—that each day I am able to love more than the day before, that I am becoming a better person each day, that in my own way I am touching and improving the lives of others. It is maintained with the conviction that the way I am spending the energies of my life makes sense . . .

This is why in a time when so many people are turning their backs on prayer, I am trying to embrace prayer with my whole being. Prayer gives me that peace. Prayer teaches me to use my life for a worthy purpose. Prayer reveals that purpose . . . Prayer fills me with hope, and that hope is not the conviction that everything will turn out well, but rather the certainty that the way I am spending my life makes sense regardless of how it turns out. Prayer allows me to live my life in peace.

january 10

WE LIVE IN a world of unlimited possibilities, but too often we get caught up in the day-to-day realities of life and the hustle and bustle of the world and lose sight of all that is possible. The busier our lives become, the more important it is to live with great intentionality. The more options we have before us, the more important it is to discern and decide with great intentionality. And living with great intentionality requires that we step back from time to time and think about life. We live more fulfilling lives when we pause each day to think about who we are, what we are here for, what matters most, what matters least, and our hopes and dreams for tomorrow.

january 11

_____

IS THERE a question that you need to answer? Is there a choice that you need to make? Is there an opportunity that you need to pursue or that you need to turn your back on? Is there a relationship that you need to throw yourself into or walk away from? What is clouding your judgment? Why all the confusion?

One way to get to some clarity is by nakedly examining your motives. Motives provide a window through which we can observe our decisions—and indecision—more closely. Sometimes it may be difficult to establish clarity about what you believe is the right thing to do in a certain situation. At these times motives can be powerful indicators. By looking honestly at the motives that are driving you toward a certain action or repelling you from another course of action, it may be easier for you to determine which direction you should take in the situation at hand.

Our motives can teach us a lot about ourselves. They often reveal what drives us, what we are afraid of, whose opinions impact our decision making, and what we consider important.

january 12

_____

FIND THAT DEEP place where you can connect with God and with the-best-version-of-yourself, a place where you can rest with God and then burst forth into the world to carry out the mission he has placed in your heart.

Reject the shallow. Learn to ponder. Learn to think deeply.

Our world has become shallow, superficial, thoughtless, and unthinking. In the midst of that, God is inviting you to live a life of contemplation; he is inviting you to think, and think deeply . . . The world needs brave men and women who will do the work to find that deep place, where they can experience union with God and live their lives from that mystical place.

january 13

A HOLY MOMENT is a moment when you open your-self to God. You make yourself available to him. You set aside what you feel like doing in that moment, and you set aside self-interest, and for one moment you simply do what you prayerfully believe God is calling you to do in that moment. That is a Holy Moment . . . This is a thing of beauty. The first line of John Keats' poem Endymion reads: "A thing of beauty is a joy forever." A Holy Moment is a thing of beauty. The poem continues, "Its loveliness increases; it will never pass into nothingness." This idea that we are discussing, this approach to collaborating with God to create Holy Moments, is a thing of beauty for two reasons. The first reason is that what we have just discussed . . . proves that HOLINESS IS POSSIBLE FOR YOU. God loves collaborating with human-ity, and if you can collaborate with God and create just one single Holy Moment, that alone proves that holiness is possible for you.

january 14

WE ARE CAPABLE of so much more than we think. You have no idea what you are capable of. None of us do. God is constantly trying to open our eyes to the amazing possibilities that he has enfolded in our being. The saints continue this work, encouraging us to explore all our God-given potential, not with speeches but with the example of their lives. When we have the courage to collaborate with God and pursue our truest self, he lights a fire within us that is so bright and warm, it keeps shining long after our days on this earth have come to an end. The lives of the saints have captivated the people of every age for this very reason.

january 15

YOU MAY BE ASKING: Why should I pray? It's a great question. It is also the answer. We have so many questions, and all too often we turn to the people around us as we look for answers, instead of turning to the one who has all the answers to all the questions. Your questions are the gateway to the answers you seek. Treasure your questions. Honor them enough to seek answers, and not just any answers. My sense is that you are not looking for generalized answered quoted to you from a book. You yearn for deeply personal answers to your deeply personal questions. The world cannot give you these. The people in your life cannot answer these questions for you, even those who know you and love you most. If you truly want to seek and find these answers, this is work for the soul. These are matters that are between you and God.

Why should you pray? Instead of giving you all the standard theological answers and reasons, I think it is more important for you find your own reasons.

january 16

_____

SEVERAL YEARS AGO, my brother Nathan was living in Japan for a year as an exchange student. During that time, I received a letter from him with a photograph he had taken of what seemed to be the courtyard of an ancient Japanese garden. In the middle of the courtyard was an almond tree in full bloom. Nathan has always been a talented photographer, but what really captured my attention was a quotation he had written on the back of the photograph. The quotation was from Nikos Kazantzakis' work Report to Greco. It read:

"I said to the almond tree,
'Sister, speak to me about God,'
and the almond tree blossomed."

Only one thing is necessary for Catholicism to flourish—authentic lives. Throughout history, wherever you find men and women genuinely striving to live the Christian life, the Church has always blossomed. If we wish to speak effectively to the modern world about God, the Christian life, and Catholicism, we must be thriving, blossoming, and flourishing in that life. The best way to speak about God is to thrive in the life he calls us to live.

YOU ARE NOT what has happened to you. You are not what you have accomplished. You are not even who you are today or who you have become so far. You are who and what you are still capable of becoming. You are your realized and unrealized potential. God sees you and all your potential, and he aches to see you embrace your best, truest, highest self. He yearns to help you and to accompany you in that quest.

Wherever you are, whatever you're feeling, however life has surprised and disappointed you, I want to remind you of one thing: The best is yet to come! There are times in life when this is easier or harder to believe, but the best is truly yet to come. Open yourself up to it, so you can see it and embrace it when it emerges!

january 18

IT HAS BEEN my experience that when you think you are there to help someone else, chances are they are really there to help you . . .

The greatest barrier to loving people, to cherishing people, and to accepting people is our inability to see ourselves in them. Take a closer look. We are one. To see ourselves in others and others in ourselves—that is wisdom.

My father always told me that the key to success in business is personal relationships. My mother always told me that the key to a rich and rewarding personal life is personal relationships. I have discovered that the key to an abundant spiritual life is personal relationship.

Life is relationship.

How are you relating?

January 19

_____

BE PRESENT in your own life. It is an amazing and rare gift. When you meet a person who has this gift, there is no mistaking it. People who are present to their own lives have this striking ability to focus on who and what is before them. They give the people and the matters at hand their complete and undivided attention. When you stand before such a person in conversation, he is able to make you feel as if no one else exists. It is just you and him. The noise around you, the people around you, even in rush hour on Madison Avenue, do not take even a breath of his attention from you and the conversation. For those few moments, it is as if nothing else exists. For those few moments, you are his life. To give his attention to anything else would be to miss something of his own life. Often we do.

January 20

WE ALL HAVE restless hearts. How often have we fallen into the trap of thinking the things of this world are more important than they are? How often have we mistakenly believed that certain things, pleasures, or experiences would make us happy for longer than they did? We have all made these mistakes, and yet God waits for us, like a patient father.

Throughout the Bible we read powerful stories imbued with relentless invitations to turn back to God. Most of us have not abandoned him altogether, but we have abandoned him in one area of our lives. In what area of your life have you abandoned God? And why? Does some area of your life seem hopeless? Have you tried time and time again to turn back to him in that area and failed? Are you ashamed of that aspect of your life? Or is there something else in your past that is holding you back?

january 21

THE TRUE CALL God is a call to personal conversion. Conversion is not a onetime experience. It is an ongoing journey. We take one step at a time. God is calling me to change. He is calling you to change. He invites me to change and grow every day, and he promises me his grace. He invites me not to become superior to other people, but to become superior to my former self. He wants myself of today to be a better self than myself of yesterday.

january 22

CONTRARY TO popular opinion, discipline doesn't stifle or restrict the human person. Discipline isn't something invented by the Church to control or manipulate the masses, nor is it the tool that unjust tyrants and dictators use to make people do things they don't want to do. All these are the lies of a culture completely absorbed in a philosophy of instant gratification.

Discipline is the faithful friend who will introduce you to your true self. Discipline is the worthy protector who will defend you from your lesser self. And discipline is the extraordinary mentor who will challenge you to become the-best-version-of-yourself and all God created you to be. As loyal and as life-giving as discipline may be, its presence in our lives is dwindling. Whether we are aware of it or not we are becoming spiritually ill without it.

january 23

HOW I WISH that when people discovered you or I are Catholic, they could immediately conclude that we are honest, hardworking, generous, loving, joyful, compassionate, temperate, humble, disciplined, prayerful, and generally in love with life. You wouldn't need too many people like this to develop a positive reputation for Catholicism in a local community. I pray that God raises them up. I pray that God will transform you and me into Catholics of that caliber.

All it will take to radically alter the way Catholics are perceived in society today is for you and me to become honest, hardworking, generous, loving, joyful, compassionate, temperate, humble, disciplined, prayerful, and generally in love with life.

january 24

WHEN I SAY the word grace, what other word comes to mind? Amazing. Grace is amazing. We need God's amazing grace. We need it badly and we need it now. Time is short, but he knows that, and I am excited to see God unleash a whole bunch of amazing grace in your life and mine, in your family and mine, in your neighborhood and mine, in your country and mine, and in our world. Amazing grace. We have all been blind and stupid at times. We have been cowards and lovers of comfort. We have been blind and lost, but all that is about to change because amazing grace is going to open our eyes so that we can see what is really happening within us and around us.

january 25

I BELIEVE the best way to defend the faith is to celebrate our faith. The best way to celebrate Catholicism is to live the faith more fully with each passing day, allowing it to reach into every corner of our lives. When Catholicism is the foundation of our family life, our social life, our intellectual life, our spiritual life, our community life, and our professional life, then we will have established an integrated life, a life of integrity. That unity of life will speak more powerfully than any words ever could. And if just a handful of people in one place and at one time will give their whole selves to seeking, discovering, embracing, and living this life, they will change the whole course of human history.

january 26

THERE IS A STORM coming. How do I know? There always is. It may be days away, weeks or months, or even years. But it is coming. Nobody passes through this life without encountering some storms. A tornado blew through our neighborhood a few nights ago. The next day seventy thousand households had no electricity, and hundreds of trees had been torn down. Other trees looked untouched. What is the difference between two trees, side by side, one gets blown to the ground and the other continues to stand tall?

Strong roots. A tree with strong roots can weather almost any storm. A tree with deep roots bears great fruit, for it can source the water and nutrients it needs from the earth. Sink the roots of the daily habit of prayer deep into your life. Is there a storm coming? Life has taught me that this is the wrong question. When will the storm get here? is more appropriate. Life has also taught me that when the storm arrives it is too late to start sinking those roots. So, don't delay. Begin today.

Prayer is life's essential daily habit.

january 27

_____

WHILE JESUS' teaching was and is radical, he calls us beyond forgiveness. One of his most radical teachings is: "Love your enemies and pray for those who persecute you" (Matthew 5:44). What was the teaching before Jesus wandered into the synagogue that morning? "An eye for an eye, and a tooth for a tooth" (Exodus 21:24).

We may have read or heard this reading from Matthew's Gospel many times. But the moment Jesus proclaimed this teaching was actually one of the great moral, ethical, and spiritual advances in human history. Jesus outlawed revenge and vengeance with one sentence.

What is he saying? He is saying love Emperor Nero, Adolf Hitler, Osama bin Laden, and child molesters, and pray for them. This teaching is so radical that when we really stop to think about it, our chests get tight, the airways to our lungs become constricted, and we find it hard to breathe.

Who are your enemies? When was the last time you prayed for them?

January 28

HUMAN THOUGHT is creative. What you think, becomes. What you allow to occupy your mind forms the reality of your life and affects the whole world for generations to come. Thought determines action. Before too long, you will be living out what has already happened in your mind. Good or bad, everything happens in your mind before it happens in reality. If you can control what happens in your mind, you can control every action of your life.

Jack Nicklaus didn't think only occasionally about being a great golfer—it was his most dominant thought for years. Cal Ripken Jr. doesn't think occasionally about being a great baseball player—it is his most dominant thought. Shakespeare didn't think occasionally about being a great writer—it was his most dominant thought. Michelangelo didn't think occasionally about being a great painter—it was his most dominant thought. Francis of Assisi didn't think occasionally about the wonder of God and His creation—it was his most dominant thought.

What is your most dominant thought? The answer to that question will tell you a lot about who you are and what you are doing with your life.

january 29

HISTORY IS FULL of examples of men and women who have become all they were created to be—we call them saints. Some of them were priests, monks, or nuns. Some were married and others were single. Some were rich; others were poor. Some were educated; others were uneducated. Some were young and some were old. Holiness is for everyone—no exceptions. Holiness is for you. Every day God invites you to be all he created you to be.

Holiness brings us to life. It refines every human ability. Holiness doesn't dampen our emotions; it elevates them. Those who respond to God's call to holiness are the most joyful people in history. They have a richer, more abundant experience of life, and they love more deeply than most people can ever imagine. They enjoy life, all of life. Even in the midst of suffering they are able to maintain a peace and a joy that are independent of the happenings and circumstances surrounding them. Holiness doesn't stifle us; it sets us free.

January 30

MOST PEOPLE overestimate what they can do in a day, and underestimate what they can do in a month. We overestimate what we can do in a year, and underestimate what we can accomplish in a decade. Whatever it is you wish to succeed at in life, personally or professionally, few skills will serve you better than the ability to take the long view.

What is the long view? It is a particular brand of wisdom that takes into account the effects that something will have not only in the present but also far into the future. The Native American people of the Iroquois have a way of making decisions that powerfully demonstrates the long view. When faced with a decision, they ponder this question: How will this proposed course of action affect our people seven generations from today?

January 31

IN CAESAREA PHILIPPI that day, Jesus asked his followers, "Who do people say that I am?" and "Who do you say that I am?" But there is a third question that doesn't appear in the sacred texts of the Gospel; nonetheless it is worthy of our consideration . . .

The third question is this: Who does Jesus say that you are?

February

February 1

GOD LOVES YOU. We all have different experiences of God and his love, and in each personal experience there are meanings and mysteries that unfold throughout our lives. I have always believed that God loves me. I'm not sure why. I don't remember anyone telling me this when I was a child, but for as long as I can remember I have believed it. Some people say that our experiences with our biological fathers have an impact on the way we see God. My own father was a good man and I grew up in his love and care, so perhaps that has something to do with it. But if I had any doubts about God's love for me, they were quickly banished when my first child, Walter Patrick, named after his paternal and maternal great-grandfathers, was born. Those first weeks following his birth were an incredibly powerful spiritual time for me. I had this awe. I remember thinking, over and over again, "If I can love my son this much, and I am weak and broken, flawed and limited, imagine how much God loves us." My imperfect love provided profound insight into God's love.

February 2

IT TAKES COURAGE to place our questions before God in prayer. It takes patience to wait for the answers, which are sometimes given to us in prayer and sometimes delivered through other people and the experience of daily life. It takes wisdom to live the answers we discover. I pray you are blessed with an abundance of courage, patience, and wisdom for the journey we are embarking upon.

I am often asked: "Why do you pray?" I pray because I cannot thrive without it. There is a much-quoted statement by Henry David Thoreau that reads, "Most men lead lives of quiet desperation." Thoreau was determined not to live such a life himself, and so, at the age of twenty-seven, he went off into the woods to live alone and reflect upon life. He remained there at Walden Pond for two years and two months. His life and writings continue to inspire millions of people to live more deliberately today. Writing about his reasons for the Walden experiment, Thoreau observed, "I went to the woods because I wanted to live deliberately. . . I wanted to live deep and suck out all the marrow of life . . . to put aside all that was not life, and not, when I came to die, discover that I had not lived."

February 3

GENEROSITY and forgiveness are two of the most radical invitations the Gospel makes. They are also among the most difficult to live.

"Whoever has two coats must share with anyone who has none; and whoever has food must do likewise" (Luke 3:11)…

Jesus wants you to become the most generous person in your sphere of influence. He wants you to astonish people with your generosity. He wants you to be generous with your time, talent, and treasure. But he invites you to a generosity that goes far beyond these. He wants you to be generous with your praise and encouragement. He wants you to be generous with your compassion and patience. He wants generosity to reach into every area of your life so that through you he can love and intrigue the people in your life . . .

Great lives belong to men and women who see life as a generosity contest. Decide right now, here, today, to live a life of staggering generosity. Astonish the people who cross your path with your generosity. There may be no more practical way to bring Christianity to life.

February 4

WHEN WE REFLECT upon our lives, we usually discover that in some ways they are functioning well and in other ways they are dysfunctional. What does this mean for you? It means in some ways you are flourishing, but in other ways you are experiencing dissatisfaction. God is speaking to you through that dissatisfaction. You can learn to live with your discontent, or you can accept it as an invitation. The danger zone is marked by comfort. This is where things aren't great, but they aren't horrible either, so you just continue to muddle along. We gravitate toward comfort, and it's amazing how comfortable we can get with things that are uncomfortable or worse. The thought of something new and unknown activates our resistance and hesitancy. These are mental, emotional, and spiritual obstacles that we all need to push through in order to move from surviving to thriving. Are you thriving or just surviving? It's time to stop muddling along.

February 5

IT'S THE ORDINARY things that God loves to elevate into extraordinary experiences. Everyone is looking for elevated experiences. God wants our lives to be filled with them. When we eat, he wants us to taste every single flavor in the food. When we drink a tall glass of clean, fresh, cold water, he wants us to be aware that it is an unimaginable miracle for one third of the world's population. When your five-year-old daughter or granddaughter comes running up to you, crash-tackles you, gives you a bear hug, and kisses you, God wants you completely present in that moment. When you take a long walk in a quiet place, swim in the ocean, make love, or bite into a crisp apple, God wants you to have an elevated experience. He gives us these elevated experiences by drawing us fully into them and filling us with a supernatural awareness of how amazing these ordinary aspects of life really are.

Our quest to create Holy Moments draws us into communion with God in the present moment, creating an explosion of awareness and joy.

February 6

"THE GLORY OF GOD is man fully alive." Some words and ideas are so powerful that they change you even as you read them. This quote, which is attributed to Saint Irenaeus, had that effect on me the first time I read it when I was fifteen. Religion and God are often accused of trying to limit people, when in reality they seek to bring the very best out of us. "Out of us" because God has already placed within us a self that is good. God and religion are often accused of trying to impose things upon people, but the reality is quite the opposite. God yearns for a dynamic relationship with each of his children, and through that relationship he seeks to draw out the-very-best-version-of-ourselves. God is interested not only in our spiritual activities, but in every aspect of our lives. He is interested not only in our spiritual self, but in our whole self: physical, emotional, intellectual, and spiritual.

February 7

SOMETIMES LIFE shakes us up a little. We become disoriented, overwhelmed, consumed by the day-to-day happenings of our lives. Britain's Royal Navy has a practice known as the "all-still." When something goes wrong on a ship, particularly a submarine, the captain announces an all-still. For three minutes, no one is allowed to move or speak. Our lives are an expression of what is within us. Life is an overflow of the heart. If within you are confused, frustrated, and exhausted, your actions will tell the same story.

Three minutes of silence and stillness can have an exponential effect in the middle of a turbulent situation. In my own life I have found that between meetings, phone calls, or in the middle of a group project, an all-still can make all the difference. It is an opportunity to catch my breath and put things in perspective.

February 8

SOMEWHERE NOT TOO FAR from where you live, someone is saying a prayer. He is asking God to send someone to visit him and lift him up out of the depths of his loneliness. His wife may have passed away and his children may live in other cities. Or maybe they just neglect him. It may be a neighbor down the street, it may be an old friend, or it may be a complete stranger whom the Holy Spirit points out to you today. Whatever the case, this person is praying to God and asking him to take away the wicked sting of loneliness. God wants you to help him answer that prayer. Visit the lonely.

February 9

THE SAINTS fixed their gaze on God. They listened to the voice of God in their lives. They resolved to cooperate with God in the fulfillment of his will on earth. They discovered their essential purpose and they fixed the attention of their thoughts, words, and actions on leading a life of holiness. They saw each moment as an opportunity to do the will of God. They knew that what God did in them was more important than anything they could ever do themselves. And as a result of these defining characteristics they blossomed and became all God had created them to be. That is the value of singleness of purpose in the Christian life, and it is written on each of their lives.

One of my favorite passages from the Bible affirms my belief that the will of God is not as much of a mystery as we make it out to be. It comes from the book of Micah, "You have been told what is good and what Yahweh wants of you. Only this, that you live justly, love tenderly, and walk humbly with your God." (Micah 6:8)

February 10

EVERY TIME YOU become a-better-version-of-yourself, the consequences of your transformation echo throughout your family, friends, business, school, neighborhood, church, marriage, nation, and beyond to people and places in the future. It is God who does the transforming, but only to the extent that we cooperate. God's grace is constant, never lacking. So our cooperation with God's desire to transform us is essential; it is the variable. Are you willing to let God transform you?

Such a simple message—yet we seem constantly obsessed with things we have no influence over, rather than focusing on where we can have most impact, which is with our own thoughts, words, and actions. It is our own thoughts, words, and actions that are at the epicenter of our circle of influence. The further we get away from them, worrying about what other people are thinking and saying or doing, the weaker our influence and impact becomes. Focus on affecting what you can affect and you will have the most effect. It all starts with you.

February 11

THROUGHOUT THE FOUR GOSPELS, Jesus speaks about money more than any other topic. The reason, I suspect, is that nothing gets between us and God like money. Nothing will mess up our values and priorities like money.

Do you have a healthy relationship with money?

There are a thousand ways to have an unhealthy relationship with money. You can hoard it or waste it, use it to control others, or lust after more of it. The list goes on and on.

There is one way to have a healthy relationship with money: Remember it is not yours. Everything belongs to God. The money and things we have he has simply entrusted to us. We are stewards.

This realization gives birth to Gospel generosity. That's right, you guessed: Gospel generosity is radical.

February 12

_____

YOU ARE NOT what has happened to you. You are not your accomplishments. You are not even who you are today or who you have become so far. You are who and what you are still capable of becoming. You are your realized and unrealized potential. God sees you and all your potential, and he aches to see you embrace your best, truest, highest self. He yearns to help you and accompany you in that quest.

Philosophers speak of "being." Anything that exists is a being. One of the most amazing things about human beings is that incredible changes can take place within us.

Your being is not fixed, stagnant, or static; it is changeable. This is a beautiful thing, primarily because from it springs endless hope.

Here is something worth pondering: The being of something changeable—you—is not only what it is, but what it still can be. You are not only who and what you are today; your essence or being also includes who you are capable of becoming—who you still can be. I love this idea. It expresses the basis for hope in our potential, and potential is a beautiful thing.

February 13

ONE OF LIFE'S most essential lessons is learning to be alone. In many ways, I believe that until we learn to be comfortable alone—and more than that, to enjoy our own company—we are not really ready to live a bold and passionate life. And until we learn this lesson we are unconditionally unprepared to be in any kind of significant relationship with another person.

February 14

IT'S TIME TO START paying more attention to your soul. Think about these four aspects of the human person: body, soul, will, intellect. We are obsessed with three of them: body, will, and intellect. We pamper our bodies, vigorously defend our right to decide the path we walk, and celebrate our individual and collective intellectual accomplishments. Yet, we often ignore the most important, soul. Have you been taking care of your soul? Rate yourself between one and ten. Most of us neglect the soul in favor of the body. When the soul is hungry, our stomach doesn't rumble and growl. But it is important to feed our soul each day. Yes, each day. How many days has it been since you intentionally fed your soul? Feeding your soul is the missing piece of the puzzle. There is no better time than right now to nurture your inner life, discover your spiritual needs, and feed your soul.

It is time to stop ignoring our souls. The soul integrates and harmonizes every aspect of our humanity. It reorients us toward what matters most.

February 15

HOLY MOMENTS come in all shapes and sizes, but the great majority of them are small and anonymous.

Begin each day with a short prayer of gratitude thanking God for giving you another day of life. Go out of your way to do something for your spouse that you would rather not do, as an intentional act of love. Offer the least enjoyable task of your day to God as a prayer for someone who is suffering. Control your temper, even if you are fully justified in losing it. Before making a decision, ask, "What will help me become a-better-version-of-myself?" Encourage someone, coach someone, praise someone, affirm someone. These are all Holy Moments.

Be patient with that person who drives you crazy. Do someone else's chores. Teach someone how to pray. Give someone a life-changing book. Ask God to lead and guide you. Tell someone your faith story. Stay calm in the midst of a crisis. Choose the-best-version-of-yourself, even when you don't feel like it. Make a healthy eating choice. Recycle. Get honest with yourself about your self-destructive habits. Tell God you trust he has a great plan for you and your life. Give whoever is in front of you your full attention. These are all Holy Moments.

February 16

URGENT THINGS often dominate the life of a parent. We rush around doing urgent things all day long. The problem with this, of course, is that the most important things are hardly ever urgent. That is why it is so important for us to identify what the most important things are and place them at the center of our lives by giving them priority. Striving to become a-better-version-of-yourself is one of the most life-giving things we can give our time, focus, and energy to, but it will never be urgent. Living passionately and purposefully is never urgent, it can always be put off for one more day—and people put it off for a whole lifetime while they obsess over all the urgent stuff. In the same way, having a great marriage will never be urgent. If we needed a great marriage to survive in the same way we need air to breathe and water to drink, I suspect there would be a lot more great marriages around. But it is not urgent, and as such, too easy to put off for another day or another year.

The best things we can do for our children are almost never urgent. For this reason, from time to time we need to step away from all the seemingly urgent things in order to

February 17

IMAGINE FOR A MOMENT that by some mysterious power you were able to change the world. What would you change? How would you change it? Perhaps you would eradicate poverty, disease, and ignorance, or put an end to war, famine, and all the useless violence and destruction that we inflict upon each other.

But changing the world is an inside-out job. When we look to change the world, too often we look outside ourselves. When God looks to change the world, he looks deep within us, driving straight to the heart of the matter: human behavior. The world is the way it is today because of human behavior. The world is changing, constantly, for better or for worse. The way we live our lives today makes it better or worse tomorrow. There are seven billion people on the planet. If your life were multiplied by seven billion, what would the world be like?

February 18

EVERY GREAT civilization since the beginning of time has concerned itself with a single question: how is the best way to live? It is the question every culture, country, generation, and individual consciously or unconsciously wrestles with . . .

The rigor with which a person or culture approaches this single question is very telling. It is of disturbing importance to note that the present culture has virtually no interest in pursuing this question. We seem more interested in how we want to live than we are in discovering the best way to live. Personal preference has triumphed over the pursuit of excellence. We want what we want, and we feel entitled to what we want.

The problem with all this is that getting what we want is certainly not work-life balance, and getting what we want almost never leads to personal and professional satisfaction. The reason is that very few people have the requisite self-knowledge to want the right things. As we grow and gain this self-knowledge we begin to want what we need because we discover that the fulfillment of our legitimate needs is more likely to lead to lasting happiness in a changing world.

February 19

_____

HOW DO YOUR BEST days begin? When I ask this question in my seminars I get many different answers: working out; having breakfast with my children; taking some quiet time for prayer, reflection, planning; getting to bed early the night before; waking up rested; giving myself enough time to get ready without rushing. The thing is, most people have never thought of it. It's a simple thing but true evidence of how little strategy there is to our lives.

You see, my own experience tells me this: if a day doesn't start as a great day, it is very, very, very unlikely to end as a great day. Once a day gets away from us, we tend to go into survival mode. Consciously or subconsciously we tend to start thinking to ourselves, "Alright, let's just get through this day!" Also, once a day gets away from you, it is very difficult to alter its momentum; it takes a lot of energy and attention to shift the energy of a day that has already gotten away from you. All this leads to the conclusion that it is best to take some time to set up a day. In doing so we give that day the best chance it has to be a great day.

February 20

PEOPLE DON'T do anything until they get inspired. But once they are inspired there is almost nothing they can't do. I often think about the disciples hiding in the upper room, scared to death, operating from a place of fear. But then the Holy Spirit comes, and boom! They are suddenly ready to go out and change the world. How? They got inspired. I mean, it was a lot more than that, and it was the ultimate form of inspiration, but inspiration was the difference.

Inspiration is the difference. Lots of people are knowledgeable, but some move men's and women's hearts, stir their souls, and inspire them to take action.

Get inspired. What inspires you? What can you do each day, each week, and each month that will keep you inspired to live in God's power? It may be time in a quiet, empty church; it may be singing in the church choir; it may be reading great books. What- ever it is, find it and cling to it. People need inspiration for their souls like they need water for their bodies.

Allow God to inspire you, to fill you with his power, because he wants to send you out to inspire others.

Who are you going to inspire today?

February 21

IN RELATIONSHIPS, we also need a common, unchanging purpose. Otherwise, relationships come unglued. You cannot have two people running in different directions and expect to hold that relationship together. You can have very different and varied interests and careers, but at the core, if the relationship is to be dynamic, successful, and lasting, it requires a common purpose. Common interests are not enough, we need a common, unchanging purpose. And the common, unchanging purpose of every relationship is to help each other become the-best-version-of-ourselves. This is true in every relationship whether that relationship is between husband and wife, boyfriend and girlfriend, brother and sister, parent and child, or between friends and colleagues. We are here to help one another become our best selves.

In a family, it is our role to help one another celebrate this common, unchanging purpose. It is not the parents' responsibility solely; it is everyone's responsibility. Even newborn babies play a role in helping others become the-best-version-of-themselves. They do it by causing people to slow down and marvel at life.

February 22

AND IF YOU and I can get even the tiniest taste of that peace—the peace that comes from knowing that who we are, where we are, and what we are doing makes sense regardless of the outcome or other people's opinions—then we have discovered our genius . . .

What is your genius? We are all capable of doing one thing better than any other person alive at this time in history. What is your one thing?

Your one thing may be to love your spouse, raise your children, or be a kindergarten teacher. Your one thing may be to invent something that changes the whole course of human history or to become the president of a great nation. It doesn't matter so much what form your genius takes as it does that you embrace and celebrate it.

How will you know when you discover your genius? There are two signs: joy and a feeling of timelessness.

February 23

WHEN WAS THE last time you paused to really think about your life? Was it last week? Last month? Last year? Or has it been a few years? Very often when I ask people this question, I see them searching their minds for an answer, and then they will say things like, "I honestly cannot tell you. I mean, I think about things that are happening in my life, or decisions that I need to make, but I can't remember the last time I purposefully made time to think about my life and how I am living it."

We are all so busy. I meet up with friends who have retired from demanding full-time jobs, and they tell me they are busier than they have ever been. Resistance loves to keep us busy. When we are too busy to reflect on how we are living our lives, it is almost certain that we are not busy doing the right things.

February 24

FOUR WORDS: Be gentle with yourself. It turns out they are some of the wisest words anyone has ever shared with me. In turn, I have shared them with many others. It doesn't mean be soft with yourself, and it doesn't mean be undisciplined. Being gentle with yourself consists of realizing your faults, failings, and weaknesses, and dealing with them appropriately. God doesn't want us to beat ourselves up. He wants us to press on and try again. In the words of Saint Francis de Sales, "Have patience with all things, but chiefly have patience with yourself. Do not lose courage in considering your own imperfections but instantly set about redeeming them—every day begin anew." One of the most important reasons to be gentle with ourselves is because if we cannot forgive ourselves, we will struggle to forgive others. And if we cannot forgive ourselves or others, we will resist even God's forgiveness.

February 25

LIFE IS A SERIES of choices. To make great choices, you must first become very clear about why you are making them. This clarity cannot be obtained in the midst of the noisy, busy world. Clarity cannot be achieved in the midst of personal chaos, whether self-imposed or not. Allow simplicity to direct your life, and permit a measure of silence and solitude to have their proper place in the course of your daily activities. Then you will catch glimpses of the-best-version-of-yourself. This vision will then guide and inspire your decisions and actions.

So much of our unrest and unhappiness comes from not knowing what to do in certain situations or how to decide in particular circumstances or what to choose when certain opportunities arise. Clarity is the great gift that simplicity brings, and clarity in decision-making is something to which we should all aspire.

February 26

THERE IS A WONDERFUL scene in Mark's Gospel where Jesus displays a beautiful human concern. "People were coming and going in great numbers, and the disciples didn't even have an opportunity to eat. He
said to them, 'Come away by yourselves to a deserted place and rest a while'" (Mark 6:31).

This is the greatest lesson in simplifying your life: Learn to say no. Many of us really have a hard time with this. For all the reasons that we have discussed, from not wanting to miss out on anything to wanting to please everyone, we really have a hard time saying no.

If your life is overcrowded, it is because you are doing more than it is right for you to do. Seek your role. Being perfectly yourself means doing only the things that are intended for you to do. You have to find your place in the grand scheme of life, but you will not find it by busying yourself with a million things that were not intended for you.

February 27

IN A WORLD where instant gratification isn't fast enough anymore, describing our society as impatient is an understatement of monumental proportions. The desire to do more, have more, and advance faster has outpaced any generation of the past. What is missing is the desire to be and become more. Who you become is infinitely more important than what you do or have. Speeding up many of life's natural processes often ends in disaster. How many people do you know who inherited a fortune? Do you think they really became who they were capable of becoming or intended to become? Probably not—and the reason is quite simple. When someone builds wealth in an ethical way, he or she develops character just by going through the process. When parents give their children the wealth, they cannot also give them the character that was developed by amassing that wealth.

Wherever you are in your career, wherever you are in your organization right now, don't despise these times. These are times for becoming, time for learning to be the-very-best-version-of-yourself, so that as more opportunity and responsibility come your way, you are prepared to succeed.

February 28

YOU ARE WHO you are, but you are also who you are capable of becoming—and you have amazing potential. You may not see it. You may feel stuck or trapped, and you may be right now. But you do not have to stay stuck or trapped. God and your potential are ready to pull you out of all that with this new habit of daily prayer.

Often when we speak of forming new habits, our motive is to look better, be more productive and efficient, accomplish more, and so on. In adopting a habit of daily prayer, these outcomes are not our goal, but you will achieve them indirectly. Peace is one of the fruits of daily prayer, and so few people have it that as you develop it, you begin to look different. A peaceful glow begins to emerge from you, and your eyes light up like never before. You will also be more efficient and accomplish more, because as you see clearly what matters most and what matters least, you prioritize your time and energy to achieve better outcomes.

Habits are incredibly powerful. They reach into every corner of our lives. This is more true for the habit of daily prayer than perhaps for any other habit.

February 29

"SMILE, say less and listen more, pray, and trust in Me, your Heavenly Father." Such a simple message. It is simple yet profound. We talk about the need for things to change in this world. Smile three times more today than you did yesterday. Say three things less today than you did yesterday and listen to three more people. Pray for three minutes more today than you did yesterday. And trustingly surrender just three aspects of your life, great or small, to God who is your Father. The world will begin to change when you begin to change.

march

march 1

DO YOU FEEL you are living your life to the fullest? I raise this question because it is impossible to confuse Jesus' invitation to "live life to the fullest" (John 10:10) with a life that is boring and meaningless . . .

It's time for you and me to start living intriguing lives. Our lives can be intriguing in really ordinary ways. It doesn't need to be man-on-the-moon stuff. If you want to intrigue people, offer them authentic friendship. Take a real interest in a small group of people's lives. Offer them care and concern. Deeply listen to them. Most people don't have anyone in their lives who really listens to them. Be that person for them. Authentic friendship has always been the key to sharing the genius and joy of Christianity with others.

Holy Moments are attractive. Holy Moments are intriguing. Holy Moments are contagious.

march 2

_____

IF IT IS IMPORTANT to spend time in the quiet, it is also important to have quiet places to go to. In the Scriptures, when we read about Jesus going off to a quiet place, it does not say he went off looking for a quiet place. It says he went off to a quiet place. This presupposes that he knew where he was going . . .

In the same way, we all need our quiet places, places we can go to when we need to step back from the world. We need quiet places set apart from the hustle and bustle of our very noisy and busy modern lives. Again, this requires some intentionality. The world draws us toward noisy places, so quiet places can be harder and harder to find. They are not going to just mystically appear at that moment in the day when we need them most. We need to plan.

I have everyday quiet places and once-a-year quiet places, and I think we need both. My everyday quiet places include a number of churches and chapels close to my home, the rocking chair out on the back porch, the leather chair in my study, and the beach. Where is your favorite quiet place? When were you last there? Should you be thinking about going there more often? How would your life be different if you did?

march 3

_____

HOW IS YOUR relationship with Jesus? Or perhaps it would help to consider some other questions. How do you wish to be known? What do you want your reputation to be? How do you want to be remembered? Would you like to be remembered for your accomplishments or for your character? Would you like to be remembered for what you did or who you were? Do you want to be remembered as a worldly person or as a spiritual person? Do you hope to be thought of as a disciple of Jesus?

We remember the saints because they had unique and intimate relationships with Jesus. Some might say they had extraordinary relationships with him, but I believe that God wants us to all have that kind of relationship with his son. God wants that kind of relationship to be ordinary and natural, carefree and unaffected . . .

In real and practical terms, what does it mean to seek first the kingdom of God? It means to enter into a life-giving relationship with him and make that friendship a daily priority. It means to keep the main thing the main thing, and the main thing is your friendship with God.

march 4

_____

WHEN WAS THE last time you said, "I don't have time!" either to an idea in your mind or to a person? What was it that you didn't have time to do? For most people it is something like spending time with the family or taking the time to look up an old friend and make sure that life is not treating her too harshly. For others it is exercise or that extra time it takes to eat properly. And at one point or another, for all of us, it is prayer. Yet if God appeared to you right now in a vision and told you that three weeks from today you would be making the journey from this life to the next, would you rush back to work to make your millions? Would you rush out to the mall to make sure you had the right clothes to die in? No. Most of us would spend time with family and friends and, in some way, try to prepare ourselves for that journey to the next life.

We do not know how long our lives on this earth will last. Some things are more important than others. Prayer, reflection, meditation, and a life with rhythm remind us of this truth and help us to remain focused on the things that are really important.

march 5

———————

SOONER OR LATER most of us arrive at a time in our lives where we say to ourselves, something is wrong. It happens to some people when they are very young and to others when they are much older. Different circumstances awaken this sense in different people, but it usually is not about the circumstances. The circumstances simply shine a light on it, but they themselves are just symptoms. The circumstances are external, but the disease is within. What we are really saying is, "This is not who I am," or "I don't feel like myself," or "I don't feel comfortable with myself," or "Who am I, and what am I here for?" or "I don't like who I've become," or "What is life really all about—because if this is all there is . . ."

These are all good and valid thoughts and questions. This moment of realizing that something is wrong is part of the process of maturing into a healthy adult human being. At these moments of enormous doubt and perplexity, you are waking up. Don't go back to sleep. Don't let someone tell you to just go back to sleep. Embrace this moment. It is the beginning of wonderful new things for you.

march 6

_____

DO YOU EVER have the sense that something is missing in your life? We all do from time to time. Most people push it aside fairly quickly, because we are afraid of where it might lead. But we really should pay a little more attention to our dissatisfaction . . .

It's okay to be dissatisfied. Being dissatisfied and pretending that we are not is the kind of lie that leads to spiritual and physical illness. Our dissatisfaction is trying to lead us to something better, or something different altogether. It is time to start listening to what God is saying to us through our dissatisfaction. I want to encourage you to pay a little more attention to that sense that something is missing in your life. This quiet discontent is creating restlessness in you for a reason . . . God is trying to tell you something.

march 7

_____

LIFE IS MEANT to be a dance for joy. But instead of participating in this dance, most of us are struggling just to survive the pressures of each day. We occupy ourselves with smaller passions, such as cooking, reading, exercising, or gardening; we throw ourselves into watching sports such as baseball or motorcycle racing or playing football or golf. We allow these smaller passions to become our focus, but by doing so, we deny ourselves the experience of much greater realities. Though we pay a good deal of attention to maintaining our physical health by eating and exercising, we humans are actually a delicate composition of both matter and spirit, body and soul. In fact, what sets human beings above other animals is the soul, which is carefully linked with the will and the intellect. Yet the soul of humanity starves. Perhaps the adventure on which I am inviting you is not the one that you have planned for your life. Perhaps this is a "different path" from the one you have had in mind. Perhaps what you read here will challenge the beliefs you currently hold.

march 8

————————

GOD, what do you think I should do?

I call this the Big Question. It is the question that changed my life forever, and it continues to transform my life on a daily basis when I have the courage to ask it. This question should be a constant theme in our spiritual lives. When we are attentive to it, we find a joy that is independent of external realities, because we have a peace and contentment within. It is the peace that comes from knowing that who we are and what we are doing makes sense, regardless of the outcome and regardless of other people's opinions. This peace comes from elevating the only opinion that truly matters: God's.

Our choices are the foundation of our lives. Every day we make dozens of decisions, some of them large and some of them small. When was the last time you invited God into the decisions of your life?

march 9

THE AUTHENTIC LIFE orients us toward the goal
of the Christian life. We are called to live holy lives, every
man and every woman without exception, regardless of our
age, color, socioeconomic background, or state in life. Living holy lives is the goal of the Christian life and our essential purpose.

We are called to live holy lives and this is something we
should strive for as Christians, but let me be very clear that
this holiness is not something that we can attain for ourselves. In truth, holiness is something God does in us and
not something we achieve. And yet at the same time, God is
the perfect gentleman: He invites us to participate in his life,
but never forces himself upon us. He wants our consent, he
wants to be invited into our hearts and lives, but much more
than consent and invitation he desires our loving cooperation. God yearns for us to be coworkers with him in this
work of holiness. It is this dynamic collaboration between
God and man that brings delight to God.

march 10

———————

YOU HAVE A DEEP need to be known. Within each of us there is a story that wants to be told. Intimacy means sharing our story. Sharing our story helps us to remember who we are, where we have come from, and what matters most. Sharing our story keeps us sane. Visit any mental institution and you will discover that most of the patients have forgotten their own story. They simply cannot put the yesterdays of their lives into any cohesive or structured memory. As a result they lose sight of the reference point that the past provides us in mapping our future. When we forget our story, we lose the thread of our lives, and we go mad. To varying degrees, we all forget our own stories, and to the extent that we do so we all go a little mad. Great relationships help us to remember our stories, who we are and where we have come from. And in some strange and mystical way, by remembering our stories we celebrate ourselves in a very healthy way. What's your story? What's your family's story? What is the story of your relationship?

march 11

_____

MOST OF the people who are at the center of the Gospel narrative have no place in our lives. What does that tell us? Jesus took people whom you and I would mindlessly pass on the street, people we would never choose to be in the same room with, people from the very margins of society, and he placed them at the center of the narrative we call the Gospel. They came to him in a hundred guises—the sick, the poor, the despised, women, children, and sinners of every type—but in each of them Jesus saw a child of God.

march 12

WHETHER YOU ARE struggling to overcome a pattern of defeat, yearning for inner peace, trying to create lasting happiness, wishing to succeed in your career, desperately trying to overcome procrastination, or battling with an addiction, this lesson holds the key for you. Just do the next right thing. In each moment, just keep doing the next right thing. You cannot think your way out or talk your way out of these problems. You acted your way into them, and you must act your way out of them. You most act in the sense of action, not in the sense of pretense. It is purposeful action that will lead you to become a-better-version-of-yourself, and action is the key to progress.

march 13

ONE OF THE great practices fostered in many spiritual traditions for thousands of years is fasting. I am not suggesting we fast completely. In fact, I am not even suggesting the strict fast of bread and water of many traditions. What I am advocating is denying ourselves in small ways so that we can regain the self-mastery that makes us free and take control once more of our temperament, appetites, and impulses.

Christians believe that through fasting they begin to reverse the way their self-destructive behaviors of the past weakened their ability to choose what is good, true, and right. We are particularly concerned with how this powerful and ancient spiritual practice might serve us in our quest to increase self-control and attain liberation from the habits of mind and body that prevent us from becoming perfectly ourselves.

march 14

NOTHING ON EARTH can satisfy your desire for happiness. The reason is very simple: You have a God-size hole. You cannot fill it with things, money, status, power, sex, drugs, alcohol, other people, experiences, or accomplishments. Only God can fill the hole. Throw all the money and possessions in the world into the hole and you will find it is still empty and you are still yearning for something more. Throw an Oscar, a Pulitzer, a Grammy or two, ten or twenty million dollars, and a Nobel Peace Prize into the hole and it will still seem empty.

We often make the mistake of hoping that certain people or things will fill the hole, but sooner or later most of us come to realize that only God can fill that hole that represents all our deepest longings. The hole is bigger than anything this life has to offer, but allowing God to fill it will make everything this life has to offer better.

march 15

_____

EVERYTHING HAS a brand on it today. What did we first use brands on? That's right: cattle. What did we next use brands on? Correct again: slaves. Do we own the brands or do the brands own us? Are we still the consumers or are we being consumed? We need to start thinking on a deeper level. Are we cattle and slaves or free men and women? God sees us as his children. He created us free and wants to keep us free. The culture sees us as cattle and wants to turn us into slaves. Do you want to be a child of God or a slave to the culture?

The problem is most of us spend a lot more time listening to the culture than we do listening to God. It's time to rebel. Rebel against the things that seek to make you less that who you really are.

march 16

_____

I BELIEVE that life should be a process of self-revelation. As we live, we reveal ourselves to the people we love and to the people who cross our path as we make our journey. We can put up barriers and put on masks, or we can let people see us as we really are.

What concerns us about the latter is that others might see our faults. In our concern, we forget that we all have faults. The people who are able to love and admire us have faults and flaws. The people who criticize and express anger and hatred toward us have flaws and failings. As human beings, one of our common bonds is our brokenness.

In truth, nobody is loved by everybody. Even the greatest men and women in history have critics. Even people who have dedicated themselves and their lives selflessly to assist others have critics and detractors. You are no different. Some people are going to like you, some people are going to love you, some people are not going to like you at all, and some people may even despise you. You might as well be yourself. That way, at least you will know that the people who like you, like you for who you truly are.

march 17

THE PRAYER PROCESS

1. Gratitude: Begin by thanking God in a personal dialogue for whatever you are most grateful for today.
2. Awareness: Revisit the times in the past twenty-four hours when you were and were not the-best-version-of-yourself. Talk to God about these situations and what you learned from them.
3. Significant Moments: Identify something you experienced today and explore what God might be trying to say to you through that event (or person).
4. Peace: Ask God to forgive you for any wrong you have committed (against yourself, another person, or him) and to fill you with a deep and abiding peace.
5. Freedom: Speak with God about how he is inviting you to change your life, so that you can experience the freedom to be the-best-version-of-yourself.
6. Others: Lift up to God anyone you feel called to pray for today, asking God to bless and guide them.
7. Finish by praying the Our Father.

Could 153 words change your life every day, forever? I have seen them change many lives; I hope yours is next.

march 18

I WAS REMINDED of a friend who had told me that the first lessons of faith come through relationships. In the care and concern I show my son, by touching him tenderly and speaking sincere words of love, I have already begun to teach him about God as a loving Father. When I go out of my way to do things for him, to help his mother, or to serve others, I am teaching him about the Eucharist, which is a powerful reminder that Jesus laid down his life for us . . . and that he calls us to lay down our lives for others.

I pray that out of all this emerges a longing to receive the Eucharist.

march 19

GOD'S DREAMS for you and me go far beyond what the world has to offer. He made each and every single one of us wonderfully unique, and he dreams that we will chase, embrace and celebrate all he created us to be: the-very-best-version-of-ourselves. Though we take pride in our individualism and independence we seem particularly enamored of fitting in. To a certain extent, the desire to fit in and be accepted is natural and normal. But when it comes at the cost of losing sight of who we are as marvelously unique individuals, something is amiss. Let us seek to discover once more what it means to be perfectly ourselves.

march 20

THE WHOLE MEANING and purpose of your existence is wrapped up in God. Separated from him, you and your life lose their meaning. About a week before Easter this year I overheard a conversation between my eldest son, Walter, who is six years old, and my daughter, Isabel, who is four.

"You are too wrapped up in Jesus, Isabel!"

"Well, Easter is all about Jesus, so it's good to be wrapped up in him," Isabel replied.

"I like Jesus, but I am more interested in the chocolate eggs and the chocolate bunnies."

Wow! There it is. Too often we are more interested in something other than Jesus, something other than the happiness that God wants to freely give us. It is only by placing God at the center of everything that we can make sense of life. Placing anything at the center of our lives other than God creates a disorientation that leads to immense confusion. This confusion has a firm grip on so many people today. If you want to make sense of everything, place God at the center of your life. Have you ever really tried it? What do you have to lose?

march 21

WE YEARN for intimacy, but we avoid it. We want it badly, but we run from it. At some deep level, we sense that we have a profound need for intimacy, but we are also afraid to go there. Why? We avoid intimacy because having intimacy means exposing our secrets. Being intimate means sharing the secrets of our hearts, minds, and souls with another fragile and imperfect human being. Intimacy requires that we allow another person to discover what moves us, what inspires us, what drives us, what eats at us, what we are running toward, what we are running from, what silent self-destructive enemies lie within us, and what wild and wonderful dreams we hold in our hearts. To be truly intimate with another person is to share every aspect of yourself with that person. We have to be willing to take off our masks and let down our guard, to set aside our pretenses and to share what is shaping us and directing our lives. This is the greatest gift we can give to another human being: to allow him or her to simply see us for who we are, with our strengths and weaknesses, faults, failings, flaws, defects, talents, abilities, achievements, and potential.

march 22

THE TRANSFORMATION of ordinary activities into prayer is the very essence of the inner life. Every activity of our day can lead us to experience God. Learn to foster the interior life in this way and you will live a life uncommon in the midst of common circumstances.

Offer the actions of your life to God as a prayer, whether you are washing the dishes, repairing a car, or studying for an exam, and by your inner intention, you will transform ordinary daily activities into the noblest tasks. By doing so, you will elevate tedious tasks to spiritual exercises that draw you nearer to God. This is how modern men and women in the midst of busy lives can seek and find intimacy with God.

march 23

PRAYERLESSNESS is one of the great torments of modern times. For decades the time we spend in focused prayer has been diminishing as our lives have become busier and busier. We have fallen into the tyranny of the urgent, which demands that we rush from one urgent thing to the next. The problem with this is that the most important things are hardly ever urgent. This can leave us always doing urgent things but never doing important things. It is these most important things that we never get around to in this cycle. Prayer is one of these important things, and among the highest priority. Prayer helps us to identify what matters most and strengthens our hearts and minds to give priority to those things in our daily lives. What could be more important than prayer?

march 24

THE VOICE OF GOD never ceases in our lives; He just uses different channels.

In more recent times during my travels I am constantly amazed at how God speaks to me through people. Whether it is a hotel attendant, someone sitting beside me on a train, an old man in a nursing home, or someone who speaks to me after one of my talks—they all share their stories with me, and in doing so they often answer questions I have been asking myself that very day. I have learned that God is wanting to give us the answers. When I was young my father used to tell me, "If you listen you will learn." He was right and I knew he was right way back then, yet I still struggle to live this truth. It is hard to listen to people, but when we do, the rewards are rich. So often we don't listen because we are too caught up in ourselves or too caught up in what we want to say.

We are always wanting to know more, yet we are often not prepared to listen. We want to know more, but we do not live what we already know.

march 25

PEOPLE DON'T fail because they want to fail. People don't go on diets to gain weight. People don't get married to get divorced. People don't join a gym and sign a two-year contract to drop out three months later.

Whether we are dealing with the area of health and well-being, relationships, finances, career or spirituality, people want to advance. We have an enormous desire to grow and change and improve ourselves. *So why don't we?* I hear you ask. *What's the problem? Why is it that so many of us seem unable to transform resolutions into habits?*

The reason most of us fail to achieve real and sustainable change in our lives is because we focus too much on the desired outcome and not enough on the progress we are making. It is important to establish goals, but they can often seem overwhelming and impossible. If we can condition ourselves to focus on the progress we are making, our advance will encourage us to persevere in achieving our goals and dreams. It is when we lose sight of our progress that we become discouraged, and it is discouragement that often lands us back in our old self-defeating habits and self-destructive behaviors.

march 26

———————

IN EACH OF US there is a Judas and a Jesus . . . It is often very easy to find the Jesus within us. Too often we shrink from the task of examining our faults. Yet it is only by knowing the flaws and defects of our character that we can begin to work to overcome them . . .

Most people don't want to know about their weaknesses. This is a classic sign of mediocrity. While the rest of us are standing around arguing for our weaknesses, trying to convince people that our lack of character is our character, the heroes, leaders, legends, champions, and saints who fill the history books went looking for their weaknesses. They didn't hide their weaknesses, and they didn't hide from them. They woke early each morning and went out to face them, because they knew their weaknesses were the keys to their richer, more abundant future.

If you want your future to be bigger than your past, start to transform your weaknesses into strengths.

Are you prepared to face the Judas in you?

march 27

EVERYTHING is an opportunity to create holy moments, to grow in holiness, and to become a-better-version-of-ourselves. Parenting is an endless opportunity, but so is being a sibling. Saint Benedict's sister, Scholastica, is also a saint. This leads us to question ourselves in a very practical way: Am I helping my siblings become the-best-version-of-themselves? Do my words and actions encourage them to love God and create holy moments?

The saints are always swirling around us, coming in and out of our lives when we need them most, and pointing out every opportunity to create more holy moments. Being a parent, being a sibling, being a spouse, work and play, friendship and community, sickness and health . . . every moment is a chance to create one more holy moment. How will you collaborate with God to create your next holy moment? Is your heart in it? Is it a wholehearted collaboration?

march 28

_____

"LET YOUR LIGHT shine before men, that they may see your good works and give glory to your Father in heaven" (Matthew 5:16).

Are you letting your light shine? There are two things I find interesting in this one verse, beyond the obvious. The obvious is that God wants you to let your light shine. The less obvious is that Jesus assumes that you will do good works. He doesn't say, "If you do good works" or "On the chance that you get around to doing some good works in the midst of your very busy life." No, he assumes that you will do good works. You were made for good works. You were created to let your light shine.

Every person lets his or her light shine in different ways. Every per- son has a perfect mix of talents and abilities. The danger here is to fall into the trap of comparisons. Comparisons are worthless in a world of individuals.

You are a perfect mix of talents and abilities to fulfill the mission that God has in mind for you. There is no point worrying about what talents and abilities other people have. If you don't have them, you don't need them for your mission. So get on out there and do good works. Let your light shine!

march 29

WHAT IS a game changer? It is an idea, a strategy, a product or service, a process or person that can create a breakthrough and take an organization to the next level.

Michael Jordan was a game changer for the Chicago Bulls. The iPod did it for Apple. The Pixar digital animation process did it for Disney. Tiger Woods was a game changer for golf. Lean manufacturing did it for the American auto industry. The idea that flying could be fun did it for Southwest Airlines. Breakfast did it for McDonald's. Cell phones and the Internet were game changers for the whole world.

The thing about game changers is that in hindsight they can seem ridiculously obvious and simple. When most people go looking for a game changer they usually spend their time and energy looking for that enormous idea that will change everything. But the reality is most game changers are small and simple. It is the simplicity of a game changer that makes implementation and broad adoption possible.

The Catholic Church in America needs a game changer. This implicitly means that most Catholics also need a game changer for their individual spirituality. I hope the four signs will be that game changer.

march 30

WE DON'T NEED more time; we need more energy.

Let's face it. There are twenty-four hours in a day. Nobody gets more, and nobody gets less. It doesn't matter how much money you have, who your father is, or how well you can kick a football. Twenty-four hours is all you get. It is probably the only way the equality we speak so much about actually exists.

The differentiating factor is energy.

Energy is our most valuable resource, not time.

For too long we have been subscribing to myths. Stress is bad. Downtime is a waste of time. Money drives performance. These are but a few.

Stress isn't bad. Stress all the time is bad. Downtime isn't a waste of time. Too much downtime is a waste of life. Money doesn't drive performance. Passion and purpose drive performance.

Energy is created by a sense of purpose and a lifestyle that integrates our legitimate needs, our deepest desires, and our talents.

march 31

_____

LIFE IS about saying yes to the things that help you to grow in holiness (become the-best-version-of-yourself) and no to the things that don't. Life is about searching each moment and discovering how that moment is inviting you to become the-best-version-of-yourself. It's disarmingly simple, but not easy. Of course, we make life a lot more complicated for ourselves by not realizing that this is what it is really all about . . .

Tomorrow, in each moment of the day, ask yourself: What can I do right now that will help me become the-best-version-of-myself? For just one day, do only those things that help you become a-better-version-of-yourself. This is the incredible vision for the human person. The reason this vision for the human person is so important is because our view on everything else flows from this primary vision . . . When our view on anything is divorced from this primary vision for the human person, our distortion of reality begins. If you start a little off course, it is amazing how lost you can become. If a plane flying from London to New York changes its direction just five degrees south, it will end up in Venezuela.

april

april 1

_____

WE ARE really good at deceiving ourselves. Most people think they are better listeners than they are; most people think they are better drivers than they really are; most people think they are healthier than they actually are; and most of us think we are better Christians than we are. We expect the truth from other people, but so often we dismiss that expectation for ourselves. It seems that we are afraid of the truth, but we needn't be. Truth is beautiful, and the truth about you is beautiful. You and I are not perfect, but we are beautifully imperfect. There is truth in that. Stop pretending to be someone you are not, living a life you are not. Stop lying to yourself. And pray for me that I can stop lying and pretending too.

april 2

IF YOU READ the writings of the great minds of every generation or study their lives and their work, you will find a common thread. They believe that beauty, truth, genius, and power is hidden in simplicity. Da Vinci, Michelangelo, Galileo, Edison, Einstein . . . all extolled the virtues of simplicity. They believed that behind all the complexity there is a simple answer to the most complex problems, and it is that simple answer that they sought. Business leaders today are searching constantly to apply this wisdom to their various endeavors. Those who rise to the top in almost any field are those who are able to break down the most complex situations and problems into a series of simple solutions. Success as a parent depends on you finding a model of simplicity and applying it to your life and the life of your family. In so doing, you will give your children not only the peace and joy that flows from experiencing simplicity, but also a blueprint for their lives.

april 3

_____

OUR LIVES genuinely improve only when we become better people today than we were yesterday; the destiny of the world is wrapped up in this deeply personal quest.

In the book of Exodus we read the story of Moses leading the people out of slavery and into the promised land. God wants to do the same for each and every one of us. He wants to lead us out of our slavery, whatever that is for you and me, and lead us to the promised land of a life filled with passion and purpose. But along the way, despite the incredible things the Lord had done for the Israelites, they turned away from God, became discontented and filled with entitlement, and began to argue among themselves and divide as a community.

What did God do? He offered them a fresh start, just as he offers each of us a fresh start today. But that fresh start was not based on ideas or philosophies. It was based on a new way of living. God invited them to change the way they behaved. He essentially said, Live by these Ten Commandments I place before you today and you will live rich, full lives in friendship with me . . . and the world will be a better place for everyone.

april 4

THE FUTURE will be what we make of it. Leadership is not an elite class. It is a role each of us is born into. It is a position of influence. Granted, some people exert more influence than others, but all of us exert some, and by our influence, people's lives are touched. People hear what you say, and they listen, and they are affected. People watch how you live, and they learn, and they are influenced.

Be a leader. Do not be afraid. Do not internalize the proclamations and criticisms of the "timid souls" and self-appointed kings of nonexistent kingdoms. When you speak to yourself, let your interior dialogue be confident, optimistic, and visionary. Dare to live the life most people only fantasize about! Do not be a destroyer of dreams, be a dreamer of dreams. Along the way, think often of Albert Einstein's words: "Great spirits have always encountered violent opposition from mediocre minds."

april 5

_____

THE AUTHENTIC life orients us toward the goal of the Christian life. We are called to live holy lives, every man and every woman without exception, regardless of our age, color, socioeconomic background, or state in life. Living holy lives is the goal of the Christian life and our essential purpose.

We are called to live holy lives and this is something we should strive for as Christians, but let me be very clear that this holiness is not something that we can attain for ourselves. In truth, holiness is something God does in us and not something we achieve. And yet at the same time, God is the perfect gentleman: He invites us to participate in his life, but never forces himself upon us. He wants our consent, he wants to be invited into our hearts and lives, but much more than consent and invitation he desires our loving cooperation. God yearns for us to be coworkers with him in this work of holiness. It is this dynamic collaboration between God and man that brings delight to God.

april 6

JUST AS the first Christians intrigued the people of their time, Mother Teresa intrigued the whole world in the last quarter of the twenty-first century. Her life announced to all men and women of goodwill that holiness is possible. Celebrated as a triumph of Catholicism by Catholics, but equally celebrated as a triumph of humanity by men and women of all faiths and those of no faith, Mother Teresa became of living, breathing, universal icon of holiness in an often cynical and self-centered world . . .

She accomplished something incredibly difficult: She reminded us of the truth, beauty and goodness within ourselves. We may be uncomfortable admitting it. We may not know quite how to activate these things in our daily loves, but Mother Teresa and all the saints invite us to keep fumbling and stumbling around with the truth, beauty and goodness God has placed within us. We may have neglected them and they may have been lying dormant within us for many years, but they still wait patiently for us to awaken them and put them to good use in our own place, in our own time, and in our own way.

april 7

———————————

SINCE MY teenage years, I have been fascinated with famous and extraordinary people—great achievers in all walks of life. I love to watch them being interviewed. I love to watch footage of their day-to-day lives. One thing that has always struck me, and I do not consider it in the slightest way to be coincidental, is that great men and women always believed that they were destined to be great. From this day on, begin to foster a belief that you were born for a reason, and although you may not have yet discovered the specifics of that reason, you are being prepared to fulfill it in every moment.

In general terms, you know that your essential purpose is to grow, change, develop, and become the-best-version-of-yourself. The details are simply that, the details. It is this process of growth that makes life interesting, exciting, rewarding, and fulfilling. Dedication to this process of growth is greatness. Greatness should never be confused with fame, fortune, status, or power. These are only passing illusions. Greatness is to become more fully your self with each passing day.

april 8

_____

WHAT WAS THE strategy of the first Christians? They lived differently, they worked differently, and they loved differently than everyone else around them. First century culture was brutal. Beyond the elite who held all the power, people were treated as objects whose main purpose was to serve the needs of the Roman Empire, whatever they might be. This cold, harsh, brutal, and deeply impersonal culture actually created the perfect opportunity or Christianity to shine and rise by contrast.

In contrast to the brutal culture of the first century, Christianity and the first Christians were warm, inviting, kind, and generous, and early Christian culture was deeply personal. The first Christians intrigued the people of their time with their selflessness in the midst of a culture where everybody seemed solely preoccupied with self-interest. That a Christian would set aside his or her self-interest to help even strangers and slaves was both baffling and appealing. The first Christians captured the imagination of their age with their love. They took seriously Jesus' directive that his disciples would be known by their love for one another and their love for others.

april 9

WE LIVE in a culture that says the meaning of life is to get what we want, and that when we get what we want, then we will be happy. We yearn for happiness because we were created for it, so we fall for the lie. We race off into the world to get what we want, but sooner or later we all realize that getting what we want doesn't make us happy.

At least not in the way we thought it would. A few months after you get that car that you wanted your whole life, it is just a car, a means of transportation. Does it bring you some happiness? Yes. Does it please and pleasure you? Yes. But it doesn't bring you that deep and lasting satisfaction that you yearn for.

Every day we make dozens of decisions, some of them large and most of them small. God wants to help you become a phenomenal decision maker. He wants to set you on fire with passion and purpose. He wants your yes to be a passionate and enthusiastic YES, and your no to be a firm NO. It is so easy to become lukewarm, but he doesn't want that for you.

april 10

_____

6.4 PERCENT of registered parishioners contribute 80 percent of the volunteer hours in a parish. 6.8 percent of registered parishioners donate 80 percent of financial contributions There is an 84 percent overlap between the two groups

At first I found these results very discouraging, but it turns out this might be the best news the Catholic Church has received in decades. Why is it good news that only 7 percent of American Catholics are highly engaged? Well, think about the tremendous contribution that the Catholic Church makes every day in communities large and small across America and around the world. Every single day we serve Catholics and non-Catholics around the world by feeding more people, housing more people, clothing more people, caring for more sick people, visiting more prisoners, and educating more students than any other institution on the planet. Now remember that all this is less than 7 percent of our capability. That is good news. If just 7 percent of Catholics are accomplishing more than 80 percent of what we are doing today, imagine what 14 percent could do. Not to mention what 21 percent or 35 percent could accomplish. Our potential is incredible.

april 11

THE IMAGE we hold of God impacts everything. Not just our spirituality, but everything. It isn't something we can sit down to discuss for an afternoon and straighten out.

There are powerful emotional, psychological, spiritual, and practical influences at work. It takes a lifetime of prayer, reflection, and observation to continually realign our image of God with the reality of who God is.

How well do you know God? I have asked myself this question many times throughout my life, and I keep arriving at the same answer: Better than I did last year, but not as well as I would like to know him.

I know this topic is just a few paragraphs in a book about prayer, but please believe me when I tell you that the implications of your personal image of God are endless. Ask God to reveal himself to you, to re-align how you perceive him with who he really is.

april 12

———————

IT FASCINATES me that if you ask a couple at their rehearsal dinner to tell their story—how and when they met, when and where the proposal took place, and so on—there is a passion and enthusiasm in the telling of the story. But as the years pass, the reply to the question "How did you meet?" becomes a three word answer, "In the library," "On a plane," "At a bar." This is a classic example of how, over time, we forget our story or become immune to its power.

Only by sharing our story with another will we ever feel uniquely known. Otherwise, and I assure you it happens every day, we can pass through this life and on to the next without anyone ever really knowing us. We also have a great need to share the story of our relationships. Just as a person who forgets his story goes insane, so does a couple who forget their story. Both participants in the relationship start to do crazy things that ultimately can lead to the breakdown of the relationship. Unless they can rediscover the thread of their relationship, unless they can remember and cherish their story together again, the breakdown of their relationship inevitably leads to a breakup, or a life of quiet desperation.

april 13

AS I BEGAN to pray more and more, the days seemed to be filled with music and the dancing never ended. The mood of the music would change. There were some slow songs, and I had to learn a few new steps, but the music never stopped. In some ways it seemed like magic, but it wasn't. It was too real, too true, while magic is merely a fraud. Yet if it wasn't magic, it also wasn't natural. It was supernatural. I was dancing for joy. The sacred was moving me.

The greater the joy and the deeper the peace, the more I desired the solitude of prayer. There was something about the silence of the time I spent each day with Jesus. I would simply sit in His presence, close my eyes, and share with Him through a conversation of the mind the things that were worrying me, my plans for the day, the problems my family and friends were having, and the blessings that filled my life, for I was starting to recognize these more than ever before.

april 14

THE DESIRE to get what we want is usually tied much more to a pleasure principle than it is to any lasting satisfaction. Too often pleasure and satisfaction are confused. The very reason Mick Jagger "can't get no satisfaction" is that he has confused pleasure with satisfaction. Many people approach the work-life balance quest in the same way.

The fundamental difference between pleasure and satisfaction is that pleasure cannot be sustained beyond the activity producing it. When we eat we feel pleasure; when we stop eating the pleasure stops. That's why we don't stop eating. We're not hungry. In fact, 75 percent of the time when we are eating we are not hungry—but we love the pleasure of eating.

Satisfaction is very different. Consider this example. You come home from work and it is your day to work out. You don't feel like exercising and would rather collapse in front of the television, but you force yourself to work out. Interestingly, whenever we get done working out we are always glad we did—even if we had to force ourselves. That's satisfaction. Satisfaction can be sustained beyond the activity producing it.

april 15

TRANSFORMING people one at a time is at the heart of God's plan for the world. It is also essential to developing dynamic marriages, loving families, vibrant Christian communities, thriving businesses and economies, and extraordinary schools and nations. If you get the man right (or the woman, of course), you get the world right.

Every time you become a-better-version-of-yourself, the consequences of your transformation echo throughout your family, friends, business, school, neighborhood, church, marriage, nation, and beyond to people and places in the future. It is God who does the transforming, but only to the extent that we cooperate. God's grace is constant, never lacking. So our cooperation with God's desire to transform us is essential; it is the variable. Are you willing to let God transform you?

If you get the man or woman right, you get the world right. Such a simple message—yet we seem constantly obsessed with things we have no influence over, rather than focusing on where we can have most impact, which is with our own thoughts, words, and actions.

april 16

———————

BEFORE WE MAKE a decision, particularly a large one (or before we give advice to assist someone else in making a decision), it is wise for each of us to take time in the classroom of silence to listen to the gentle voice within. Silence and solitude give a perspective to the situations of our lives that could not be gained by a thousand hours of conversation or a thousand pages of books.

Yet this thoughtful reflection also cannot take place in a vacuum. It must take place in relation to the space and time of our everyday lives by considering the matter at hand in light of our hopes and dreams, and with our essential purpose ever before us.

If you do not know where you are going, you will never get there . . .

Knowing who we are (strengths, weaknesses, needs, talents, and desires) and what we are here for (to become the-best-version-of-ourselves) is the knowledge that liberates us from the modern enslavement of a life of meaninglessness and gives our lives back to us once more.

april 17

THE SCRIPTURES are full of references to the Eucharist, but many people find the leap from these words to the reality of the true presence too daunting. Nonetheless, if you have doubts or disbelief, set them aside for a moment. Suspend your judgment, and imagine it is real. Imagine you could receive the body and blood of Jesus Christ under the guise of bread and wine. Imagine the Catholic experience of the Eucharist is what Jesus had in mind. Imagine how that might transform you. Imagine how receiving the Eucharist might empower you to become more perfectly the person God created you to be. Imagine how that realization would allow you to go out into the world and set it on fire. Imagine if each time we received Jesus in the Eucharist we became a little bit more of whom and what we received. Imagine . . .

There is power in the Eucharist. It is Jesus who walked the earth as our teacher—the same Jesus who died, rose from the dead, and ascended into heaven as our Savior. It is the glorified Jesus who transcends time and space. He is the healer of my soul . . . and he yearns to be the healer of yours.

april 18

_____

THE NORTH STAR is the only star in the sky that never moves; it remains constant and unwavering, and therefore is a true guide. In the same way, God's call to live a holy life never changes. In a world of rapid and constant change, it is what is unchanging that allows us to make sense of change. The ideas you encounter may change, your emotions may change, but God's call to live a holy life never changes. The North Star of the spiritual life is the call to holiness. It leads us unfailingly to Jesus, who is "the Way, the Truth, and the Life," even when he seems distant or unknown. If we are to find our way as individuals and as a Church, it is vital that we rediscover this great spiritual North Star, so that in times of confusion or decision we can ask ourselves, "How is this situation an invitation to grow in holiness?"

Holiness and renewal are inseparably linked. Where there is holiness the Church has always thrived. If the Church is not thriving there is one primary reason for that . . . and when you and I begin to take God's call to live holy lives seriously, the Church will begin to thrive in new and exciting ways.

april 19

_____

PRIMARY and secondary relationships have a way of influencing each other. Pleasant and unpleasant things happen to us every single day of our lives. Great relationships magnify the good things that happen to us and make the unpleasant things bearable.

When something wonderful happens to you, who are the first people you want to tell? When tragedy strikes, which people do you want to be with? Whom do you want at your bedside keeping you company when you are sick? Who encourages you when you fail? Who challenges you gently to succeed? Whose life do you want to significantly impact with your life?

Life is a limited experience, and yet, there is an unlimited number of people, places, and things to experience in your limited time. In the arena of relationships, we also have a limited amount of time and unlimited opportunities. There are almost six billion people on the planet; you cannot have a personal relationship with each of them. You must choose.

april 20

THE MESSAGE of the world is incomplete, and nothing demonstrates this incompleteness more than the world's inability to make sense of suffering. The world cannot make sense of suffering because it views suffering as worthless. The world has no answer for the inescapable, unavoidable, and inevitable suffering of our lives. Jesus has an answer for everything . . .

In the New Testament, Jesus boldly announced with his words and actions that suffering has value. It is a tool that can transform us into more loving people. It ushers us into higher spiritual realms. Salvation and the suffering of Jesus are inseparable. So what could be more meaningful than suffering? . . .

"If any want to become my followers, let them deny themselves and take up their cross daily and follow me" (Luke 9:23). The mandate is clear. I don't know what your cross is, but I sure know what my own is. Some days I am more reluctant than others to pick it up and carry it. That's life. What cross is Jesus inviting you to take up and carry today? Whatever it is, the risen Christ wants to help you carry it. You are not alone.

april 21

———————

OUR CORE BELIEFS . . . guide us in times of uncertainty and confusion. They allow us to thrive in the midst of constantly changing environments at home, at work, at school, in relationships, and in society. That is why it is so important that we take time to step into the classroom of silence on a regular basis and reflect on what matters most and what we believe. Only then will we be able to keep the counsel of the voice of the authentic self that whispers to us night and day from within . . . and only then will we begin to establish the unity of life that gives birth to integrity, inner peace, and enduring happiness.

It is one thing not to believe something; it is something completely different and debilitating to believe and not live in that belief. Old-fashioned as it may seem to people, there is a lot of restlessness and disease in our lives that could be quickly cured by a clear conscience. Let us start to live all the good things we believe.

april 22

THE MASTERY of almost anything is about the basics. As human beings, we are fascinated with things that are new and different, special or extraordinary, the latest shiny, sparkly things. But almost all success and happiness in this world is born from ordinary things. We allow ourselves to be seduced by the spectacular, but the basics are where you find the true and lasting treasure.

Success at almost anything rests upon this single principle: Do the basics, do them well, and do them every day, especially when you don't feel like doing them. It doesn't matter if it is football, marriage, parenting, personal finances, physical fitness, military operations, small business, big business, or prayer. This is one of the reasons most people don't become phenomenally successful. They lack the persistence to do the same things over and over again.

Mastering the basics is the secret to success. So as we make this journey together, resist the temptation to look beyond the basics. Throwing yourself into the basics day after day may get tedious from time to time, but the peace and joy that come from an established habit of daily prayer never do.

april 23

———————————

WHAT IS CAREFREE timelessness? It is time together. Not five or ten minutes, but two hours or four hours, or a weekend away. And it isn't just a lot of time together. Carefree timelessness is time together without an agenda.

All relationships thrive under the condition of carefree timelessness, but we don't gift our relationships with carefree timelessness. We try to shove them into five minutes here and ten minutes there, a cell phone call here and an instant message there. Do we actually expect that our relationships can genuinely thrive under these conditions? Do we sincerely feel that this is enough to form a significant connection with another human being? Or have we simply failed to think about it, because we are distracted by the everyday insanity of our busy lives?

april 24

———————————

GOD WANTS you to be happy even more than you want it yourself. Imagine how frustrated God is with us, seeing all that is possible and knowing how we squander so much. But he will not cross the line. He will not step over your free will. God wants to empower you for mission. He has put you in this world for a specific mission, but first he has to prepare you.

april 25

———————

WHAT IS THE MEANING of life? What are we here for? What is the purpose of our existence? Modern popular culture proclaims directly and indirectly every day that life is merely a pleasure-seeking exercise. "If it feels good, do it" seems to be the credo. It is this same voice of popular culture that creates the confusion between sex and intimacy, between common interests and a dynamic relationship, and that perpetuates a thousand other myths and illusions that lead men and woman ever deeper into the despair of purposelessness. There is nothing more depressing than not knowing your purpose.

Our essential purpose is to become the-best-version-of-ourselves. This one principle will bring more clarity to your life than all you have ever learned put together—and, more than that, it will help you to live and celebrate all the great wisdom you have learned in your journey so far.

Everything makes sense in relation to our essential purpose.

april 26

WHEN YOU SEE this holiness alive in a person, even for a moment, it is inspiring. The truth is, virtue is ultimately attractive. When Jesus walked the earth, people wanted to be with him. Whether he was speaking in the synagogue, walking down the street, or eating at someone's home, people wanted to be with him. They crowded around him, hung on his every word, grasped just to touch his cloak. There is nothing more attractive than holiness. This attractiveness has not only been demonstrated in Jesus, but is constantly demonstrated here and now in our own place and time: whenever someone goes out of his or her way to ease the burden of a stranger; whenever someone is honest; whenever someone lays down his or her life by working hard to support his or her family; whenever someone rejects the premise of modern culture. Not only is holiness attractive; it is inspiring and intriguing to the people of any era. It is also immensely practical. When you hear that the doctors and nurses at a local hospital are coaching the inner-city baseball teams, doesn't it fill you with hope? What is holiness? Holiness is all the incredible things God will do in you and through you if you make yourself available to him.

april 27

———————

THE SENSATION we call love can expand or contract. It expands when it is nurtured and contracts when it is neglected. Dynamic relationships require effort and self-sacrifice and thoughtfulness, and if you and your partner are willing to bring these things to the table, your experience of love can expand endlessly and infinitely.

Infinite expansion is possible, but not in an infinite number of relationships. You have only so much time and energy, so you have to decide which relationships matter most. You have to be willing to opt out of certain relationships in order to give your most important ones the time and attention that they require and deserve.

april 28

_____

IT WAS BY reflecting on my past that I began to develop trust. As I prayed, I recalled the way the pieces fit together in the kaleidoscope of my past; as I looked back, it was clear that there had been a "Planner." In this way, I learned to trust the Planner and realized that He was my Father and the Father of all of humanity. Our Father.

It quickly became apparent that my Heavenly Father had a plan for my happiness. In this plan my happiness and victory were assured. He called me to prayer so that He could open my eyes to the plan. As I slowly awakened to the realities of the spirit world, I began to see that nothing was a coincidence, that everything fit perfectly into a much greater plan than any of us could formulate in our own little minds. The plan was Divine.

Nothing in this life is a coincidence. There are no accidents, just providence. Providence, providence, all is providence. Our happiness comes from seeking, finding, and struggling to live in harmony with this plan. The plan is truth, but it will never be imposed upon us. No one can force you to be happy.

april 29

THE CRITIC will always be present.

I was watching a short Winnie the Pooh film online with Walter last year, and at the end of the film you had the opportunity to like or dislike it. The film had thirteen million likes and twenty-five thousand dislikes. And I thought to myself, "It is a classic story, a classic character—and what's not to like about Winnie the Pooh?" But twenty-five thousand people disliked it enough to voice their opinion. Even poor Pooh has haters.

The critics will always be there, but it is not the critic that counts. Have you ever seen a statue of a critic? No. I haven't either. Do they award any Nobel Prizes for Critic of the Year? No, there is no Best Critic Ever statue or award.

We live our lives for an audience of one: God. If you are doing what you believe God is calling you to do deep in your soul, walk on.

april 30

ALBERT EINSTEIN wrote, "I want to know the thoughts of God. Everything else is details." I hope my son develops an intimate friendship with God, a curiosity about the Divine, an appreciation for all things spiritual, and an understanding of Jesus Christ—the turning point of human history.

In all my life I don't think I have held such a lofty ambition as that of passing the faith onto my children. How will it be achieved? What can I do to bring it to fruition? Is it within my influence or beyond it?

And while I ponder these questions, I know it is impossible to ignore the unprecedented exodus taking place at this time as men and woman of all ages leave the Catholic Church. Where do they go? Some are drawn to the allure of nondenominational megachurches. Many just stop going to church altogether. Why do they leave? I suspect it is a combination of factors. Even the most casual observer would conclude that two of those factors seem to be that they don't know what they are leaving and that the Church failed to speak into their lives in a way compelling enough to engage them.

may

may 1

_____

THIS CONCEPT of celebrating the-best-version-of-ourselves at different moments and in different situations throughout the day brings the philosophical question about the best way to live to a very real and practical level. As our awareness grows we become mindful that we are constantly making choices and that every choice causes us to become a-better-version-of-ourselves or a-lesser-version-of-ourselves.

If we accept the first principle, then the meaning-of-life conversation becomes a fairly short one. You are here to become the-best-version-of-yourself. We all have this in common, so the best way to live, on a macro level for everyone, is by making an effort to become the-best-version-of-ourselves. Thus, on one level the answer to the question "How is the best way to live?" is the same for us all.

may 2

THE MODERN WORLD is a complex world, and the problems our world faces are complex problems. So the temptation is to turn to complexity for answers to these complex problems. But the answer is not more complexity, and the solutions to our complex problems are much simpler than we seem willing to realize. We have become hypnotized by complexity, but the essence of Christianity is simple. In that simplicity, Christianity is good and beautiful, positive and hopeful. Goodness, beauty, and hope—these are things that people need. They are things that I need. And if you and I don't allow these things to flow through us into the world, then who will? When will they? And can the world and all the people trapped in misery wait? I think not. I think now is the time. Now is our time.

may 3

_____

THE FOUR SIGNS can manifest themselves in different ways from one person to the next. But imagine for a moment if everyone in your parish did these four things:

1. Spent ten minutes each day in prayerful conversation with God
2. Read five pages of a great Catholic book each day
3. Gave 1 percent more of their income to support the mission of their parish than they did last year
4. Did one thing each week to share the genius of Catholicism with someone else.

How would your parish be different after one year? How would it be different ten years from now?

Prayer, Study, Generosity, and Evangelization. It is a simple plan, but complex problems demand simple solutions. It is the simplicity that allows widespread adoption and participation.

may 4

_____

THE FUTURE passes by way of the family. Every man and woman on this planet has been influenced for better or worse by the family he or she was born into. It is an influence that we still do not quite understand and it is an influence that is inescapable. Children whose mothers abandoned them at birth spend their whole lives trying to understand how that may have affected them. Children whose mothers give them up for adoption do the same. Children born into loving families where the father or mother works too much visit therapists every day trying to understand the inexplicable. The examples and stories are endless. Families have an enormous influence on our lives.

Beyond the personal impact our family circumstances have on us, sooner or later we need to step back as a society and ask ourselves: What impact is our family culture having on our future as a society and nation? Family is a deeply personal experience, but it is one that echoes throughout our lives and down through history. Raising children is a deeply personal endeavor, but it is one that sends waves of love or hatred, virtue or vice, selfishness or generosity down through history.

may 5

_____

"YOUR THOUGHTS are not my thoughts, nor are your ways my ways, declares the Lord" (Isaiah 55:8). It is interesting that a connection is made here between thoughts and action. What we spend our days and weeks thinking about has an enormous impact on our actions.

What are you thinking? As you make your way to work each day, as you are waiting in the doctor's office or standing in the grocery store line, in those moments between activities, what do you think about?

I know this for certain: Whatever we spend these apparently inconsequential moments thinking about will increase in our lives. Few things will have more impact on your life than what you allow to occupy your mind. Use these times to ponder the ways of God and you will find yourself living them.

may 6

_____

WHAT GREAT LESSONS can nature teach us about ourselves? Nature whispers messages to us each and every day: "Great things are achieved little by little. Discover the rhythm of life and align your life with this rhythm. The more you do, the more you will enjoy peace and prosperity."

The truth of this message is displayed all around us in thousands of ways every day. The waves roll onto the shore, washing against the rocks, and erosion occurs. You do not see it with the first wave or with the second or third, but over the years you realize that slowly and steadily the waves are wearing the rock down. Who would think of water as stronger than rock? Persistence has strength.

The rhythm of life is a powerful thing.

may 7

_____

THE LESSON I learned was that someone can look perfectly fine, but you never know what is going on inside—and everyone has something going on inside.

Most people can hide it pretty well and get on with whatever the day requires of them so that they can support their families and raise their kids, or keep their schools, churches, businesses, or hospitals running. But it doesn't change the fact that each of us in our own way is grappling with something.

What hard battle are the people who live under the same roof as you wrestling with? What hard battle are the people you work with fighting? When we recognize that someone else is fighting a hard battle, we tend to rise to the occasion. It brings the best out in us, and compassion and generosity begin to flow. So next time somebody is upsetting you, frustrating, annoying, or ignoring you, take a deep breath and remember that she is fighting her own hard battle. Allow the greatness of your humanity to rise up within you, and act with compassion.

may 8

IT IS NATURAL to have doubts, but we have a responsibility to seek out the truth that will assuage our doubts. Raise your questions, but don't expect other people to serve you up answers on a silver platter. Doing the work to find answers to your questions is an important aspect of the spiritual life. Answers easily found are often easily discarded. Seeking answers to our personal questions and wrestling with our doubts helps us to build a more robust faith . . .

Healthy faith asks questions. The important thing to keep in mind is motive. What motive is driving your question? Are you really looking for answers or are you look for an excuse not to believe? The former will grow your faith; the latter will destroy it. Investigate your doubts by all means, but do it with a hunger for truth.

may 9

_____

SELF-CONTROL is always accompanied by self-aware-
ness. As we become more and more aware of ourselves and
of the way we react to certain types of people and situations,
our ability to control our response increases. The moment
between event and response is where we choose how we
are going to react. People with short fuses are almost completely oblivious to the moment because their temper-filled
reactions have shortened with practice.

A short temper is a habit that has been chosen and can
be changed. Anger is a natural and normal part of our human makeup. I think people love the passage in the Bible
where Jesus goes into the temple and turns over the money
changers' tables. It reveals a very human side of Jesus that
people can relate to. There are times when anger should be
expressed and expressed powerfully. But they are rare. Like
any passion, for anger to be useful it has to be harnessed,
controlled, and directed at will.

The Psalms and Proverbs have plenty to say on this topic.
"A fool gives full vent to his anger, but a wise man quietly
holds it back" (Proverbs 29:11). "Set a guard over my mouth,
O Lord, keep watch over the door of my lips" (Psalm 141:3).

may 10

_____

FEW THINGS will impact our experience of prayer more than the image of God we hold in our hearts. The difficulty is we each have an incomplete and distorted image of God. The Scriptures teach us that we were created in the image of God, but without authentic experiences of God the danger is that we begin to create God in our image. Through the daily habit of prayer and other spiritual practices, our image of God gradually becomes more aligned with the reality of who God is.

What is your image of God? How do you envision God? Do you imagine God as a loving father or as a wrathful father? Do you see Jesus as a teacher, brother, friend, Savior?

Do you envision the Holy Spirit as close and personal or distant and impersonal?

may 11

"THE GLORY of God is the perfection of the creature." The human person is perfected by the grace of God through the conscious, disciplined, and persistent attainment of virtue. But the grace of God is never lacking, so it is our conscious, disciplined, and persistent effort that is the key to a richer and more abundant future for humanity. This disciplined striving for virtue is an indispensable characteristic of the authentic life.

It is important to understand that the perfection that God calls us to is not some type of robotic perfection. Your big ears and your bent nose are a part of your perfection, but the defects in your character are not part of your best self.

God wants you to be holy. Your holiness is the desire of God, the delight of God, and the source of your happiness. To embrace who you were created to be and to become the-best-version-of-yourself is God's dream for you. Therefore, holiness is for everyone, not just for a select few, for monks in monasteries and nuns in convents; it is for you and me.

.

may 12

———————

WITH EVERY CHOICES, we can improve our relationship or diminish it. When faced with a choice, when an opportunity presents itself, whenever we have a decision to make, the first question we need to ask ourselves is, "Which of the opportunities before me will help me become the-best-version-of-myself?"

By constantly asking this question in the moments of the day, and then by living the answer, we place our essential purpose at the center of our lives and at the center of our relationships.

At the breakdown and breakup points of relationships, I often hear people say, "Nothing makes sense anymore." Why doesn't anything make sense anymore? Nothing makes sense anymore for these couples because they have lost sight of the essential purpose of their relationship. In many cases, they were never consciously aware of this great purpose. They may have enjoyed a mutual pleasure or some commoninterests, but their relationship never matured to include the great ambition of extraordinary relationships— the pursuit of our essential purpose.

may 13

GOD HAS A PLAN for each of us, but He perfectly respects our personal freedom, our ability to choose for Him or against Him, our ability to choose life or death, our ability to choose happiness or unhappiness.

"I know the plans I have for you, says the Lord, plans for good and not evil, to give you a future and a hope." (Jeremiah 29:11)

Clearly and absolutely, the only thing that matters at the end of the day is whether we have cooperated with this plan.

Our individual correspondence with the plan develops inner harmony as well as world unity and peace. If we want to live in a peaceful world, we must first realize that we will never achieve this peace and harmony while the battles are still raging in our own hearts.

If it is in the plan that you will live, then you will have air to breathe.

To breathe is not a right; it is a gift.

may 14

_____

THE TRUTH IS, people are walking around half-asleep all the time. Every day, people are exhausted. They are fatigued. Fatigue has become a pattern in our lives. This is a sad testament to how little we observe, know, and respect ourselves.

When was the last time you woke up and felt renewed, refreshed, and excited to get into your day? That is what I want you to experience—not occasionally, but every day . . .

Being rested is not just about being awake—it's about being able to devote yourself completely to whatever is before you in every single moment of the day. It is about living life to the fullest.

_____

AVOIDING TRANSFORMATION has a very real impact on our spirituality. Once we abandon the transformation that is the Christian life, our focus falls on tweaking; our spirituality becomes mediocre and very self-centered. Then we start praying for tweaking: Dear God, please tweak this . . . and please tweak that . . . and tweak my spouse . . . and tweak my spouse again because it didn't take the first time . . . and tweak my kids . . . and tweak my boss . . . and tweak my colleagues at work . . . and tweak my son's soccer coach . . . and tweak my daughter's schoolteacher . . . and tweak our pastor . . . and tweak the politicians . . .

We pray for tweaking—and then we wonder why God doesn't answer our prayers. The reason is simple: God is not in the business of tweaking. He's in the business of transformation.

may 16

THE HEROES, champions, and saints who have exemplified Christian living for two thousand years did not live holy lives. It is a mistake to step back and look at their lives and say, "She lived a holy life" or "He lived a truly holy life." And these men and women that we place on pedestals would be the first to admit that they did not live holy lives—they lived Holy Moments. Their lives were not a single action. Rather, they lived life like you and I, one moment at a time. Did they collaborate with God to create Holy Moments? Yes. Did they turn their backs on God at other times and create unholy moments? Absolutely. In fact, it is essential to note that between all the Holy Moments these champions of Christianity were creating with God, they did some really sick, crazy, dark, twisted, demented, and messed-up stuff. Take Paul the Apostle as an example. We are talking about a guy who hunted down Christians to murder them. If he didn't murder them himself, he was certainly complicit and gave the orders to have them imprisoned, tortured, and murdered. I don't know about you, but this gives me great hope.

may 17

_____

A PITCHER of doesn't throw a hundred-mile-per-hour fastball on his first attempt. First he learns to hold the ball, then he learns to throw the ball, and then he learns to throw the ball in the right direction. He throws a seventy-mile-per-hour ball before he throws an eighty-mile-per-hour ball, and a ninety-mile-per-hour ball before he throws that hundred-mile-per-hour fastball. There may be days when he can't throw as fast as he could the day before. In these moments, he must either celebrate his overall progress or focus on some aspect other than speed. He is not throwing as fast, but perhaps he is moving the ball better than he ever has or throwing with more accuracy. At every juncture, he celebrates his progress.

When a pitcher gets injured, he begins rehabilitation by going back to basics. He returns to the beginning, even to such fundamentals as learning to hold the ball again. A great rehab coach designs a plan with stages and goals along the way so that the recovering athlete can celebrate his progress.

Celebrating progress is fundamental in the psychology of change. Celebrating progress is the first secret to breaking those patterns of failure.

may 18

_____

FOR ALL THE PEOPLE who have left the Catholic Church over the years, I don't know a single person who has left who believes in the true presence. It is what sets the Catholic Church apart from all modern forms of Christianity.

If I reflect upon the gift of faith that I have been given, I am led to the conclusion that once we believe in the Eucharist we are given the grace to look beyond a bad homily and the grace to look beyond a good homily, the grace to look beyond uninspiring music and the grace to look beyond music that elevates our hearts, minds, and souls. For it is beyond all these things that we find Jesus in the Eucharist.

Of course, it is not an easy teaching to believe. Jesus said, "I am the bread of life. . . . Unless you eat the flesh of the Son of Man and drink his blood, you have no life in you. Whoever eats my flesh and drinks my blood has eternal life, and I will raise them up on the last day."

How did the people of his time react to this teaching? "On hearing it, many of his disciples said, 'This is a hard teaching, who can accept it?'" Isn't that exactly what so many people say now, two thousand years later?

may 19

RAISING AMAZING children is a full-time job. If it was the only thing you had to do, you would still not have enough time to do it to the best of your abilities. Parenting, like most things in life, is about making the best of limited resources. You do the best you can with what you have where you are. There are no perfect parents, but some are better than others. The best ones are dedicated to contiuous improvement. They don't read a book about parenting and make it their Bible on the subject. They read many books about parenting, history, business, relationships, and any other number of subjects. They talk to friends at work, at school, and at church. They listen to audiobooks and attend seminars both personally and professionally. They see movies and listen to music. They eat and exercise and make love. In short, they live their lives. And as they do, they pause after daily experiences and ask themselves: What did I learn from this that can make me a better parent to my children?

may 20

THE TRUE CALL of God is a call to personal conversion. Conversion is not a onetime experience. It is an ongoing journey. We take one step at a time. God is calling me to change. He is calling you to change. He invites me to change and grow every day, and he promises me his grace. He invites me not to become superior to other people, but to become superior to my former self. He wants myself of today to be a better self than myself of yesterday.

may 21

_____

JESUS INVITES us to a total love of God and a generous love of neighbor, but he assumes that we already love ourselves. "You shall love your neighbor as yourself." There is a connection between our ability to love ourselves in a healthy way and our ability to love our neighbor. This is a major stumbling block for many of us as Christians. It is a generalization, but my experience leads me to conclude that many Christians do a horrible job of loving themselves . . .

I am not speaking of the love of self that is blind and boastful, but rather the love of self that acknowledges that we are weak and wounded, and at the same time that we are amazing children of God. It's that unique combination of humility and gratitude that allows us to acknowledge (even if we don't understand it) that God loves us deeply, that he loves us for a reason, and that that alone is proof that we are lovable.

We are lovable. You are lovable.

may 22

IF YOU CAN'T measure it, you can't change it. Measurement is key to personal growth and integral to parish growth. Certainly, there are some things that are very difficult to measure—how generous you are with your patience or forgiveness, for example. There are other things that are very easy to measure, such as how generous you are with your money. But there is something that holds all these together. It is unlikely that those who are unwilling to be generous with their patience or forgiveness will be generous with their money. Similarly, if we are not generous with our neighbor it is unlikely that we are generous with God. There may be many ways to express our generosity, but they are all interconnected and flow from one heart.

Is God calling you to live more generously? I have never asked this question and heard no as the answer. Every time I ponder this question God challenges me to a greater level of generosity— not because he wants me to give all my time, talent, and treasure away to others, but because he wants me to live a free and happy life. The happiest people I know are the most generous people I know, and they seem free from the things of this world in a way that is to be admired.

May 23

WE ALL KNOW too well from our experience in other areas of life, whether it is business, science, or sports, that without clearly defined goals, little is achieved and most people grossly underachieve. This was Michelangelo's observation: "The greater danger for most of us is not that our aim is too high and we miss it, but that it is too low and we reach it."

I believe there is a direct relationship between happiness and holiness. This was my first serious observation of the Christian life as a teenager. I must also confess it was the reason I first began to explore Catholicism seriously. As simple as it may sound, I was aware of my yearning for happiness. I had tried to satisfy this yearning in other ways and had been left wanting. I had witnessed a peace and purpose in the lives of a handful of people I knew who were striving to live their faith, and I knew they had something I was yearning for.

My experience of people and life continually teaches me that those who have no central purpose in their lives fall easy prey to petty worries, fears, troubles, and self-pity. I have also learned that those living authentic lives simply try to be all they can be, here and now, and that brings with it a happiness all its own.

may 24

_____

IN HIS FIRST LETTER to the Thessalonians, Paul addresses this same question, writing, "This is the will of God: that you be saints." (1 Thessalonians 4:3) God wants you to be a saint and it is critical for modern Catholics to hear this call to sanctity. We all need to be reminded that holiness is possible. The will of God can be discovered and embraced, and this is a truth that both encourages and challenges us at the same time. But in order to allow this truth to animate our lives, we need to set aside our prejudices against the idea of holiness and embrace a new vision of what it truly means.

WHEN WE BEHAVE in ways that are contrary to our values, beliefs, and principles, the result is inner conflict and shame. We then have to either resolve the inner conflict by living in accord with our values, beliefs, and principles in the future, or else flee from our shame. Flight from shame is of course impossible, because in a very real way it is an attempt to flee from ourselves. The story of many people's lives can be summarized into two parts: the betrayal of self and the flight from shame. For once we betray ourselves we run unceasingly from our shame, unless we can summon the humility to face our error and begin anew.

Guilt and shame serve to warn us when our behavior is inconsistent with what we hold to be good, true, and just.

Never did William Shakespeare pen truer words than the day he wrote: "To thine own self be true, / And it must follow, as the night the day, / Thou canst not then be false to any man."

may 26

SO, WHAT IS God really like? God has many attributes. He is infinite, eternal, good, self-sufficient, ever-present, generous, holy, personal, gracious, loving, wise, mysterious, all powerful, one, providential, righteous, just, transcendent, truthful, eternal, and deeply interested in everyone and everything he has created. From time to time, I like to ask myself: What are three attributes that most help you connect with God? These are the three I picked today: loving, patient, and faithful. At other times in my life, I have chosen other attributes. I chose loving because love seems to be the essence of everything that God is and does, and I yearn for it to be the essence of who I am and all I do. But on a more basic, human level, I yearn to love and be loved. I chose patient because I know my faults, failings, and limitations, and I need him (and anyone I am in relationship with) to be patient with me as I fumble around trying to become a-better-version-of-myself. I chose faithful because I need to remind myself that our God keeps his promises. I find this to be a great reminder and comfort in times of trouble or uncertainty. What are the three attributes that most help you connect with him?

GOD CALLS each of us to holiness. He invites us to be truly ourselves. This call to holiness is in response to our deep desire for happiness. We cry out to God, saying, Show us how to find the happiness our hearts are hungry for, and God replies, Walk with me, be all I created you to be, become the-best-version-of-yourself. It is a natural and logical conclusion that we will never find happiness if we are not ourselves. Imagine if a bird tried to be a fish, or if a tree tried to be a cloud. No matter how hard a bird tried to be a fish, it would never succeed. The challenge life presents to each of us is to become truly ourselves—not the self we have imagined or fantasized about, not the self that our friends want us to be, not the self our ego would have us be, but the self God has ordained us to be from before we were in our mother's womb. The authentic life manifests itself differently in every person through our needs, talents, and desires. Get in touch with your essential purpose—to live a holy life—and once you have found it, keep it always in your sight. This is the great spiritual secret of life.

may 28

PERHAPS IT'S TIME we did some great service to humanity again. I know, we do a great service to humanity every day. But perhaps it is time for something bigger, something bolder . . .

If over the next decade the Catholic Church decided to end child poverty in America, we could do it. It's just one idea, and maybe it's not the right one. But here's the thing: Who is going to criticize the Church for trying to end poverty among children in America? We need to do something big and bold, something that everyone can agree is a good thing, whether they are Catholic or not. We need to change the conversation if we are going to engage the people of our times . . . If together Catholics announced that we are going to put an end to child poverty in America by the end of the decade, it would energize people and mobilize them. People follow bold missions. They want to give their lives to something bigger than themselves. We should be able to present them with a vision that inspires them to throw themselves into it with reckless abandon. The Catholic Church in America is waiting to be reinvigorated. The whole world needs to be reintroduced to the love and wisdom of Jesus Christ. These two realities are connected.

may 29

———

THE CLOUDS do not need to open and lightning to strike for God to speak. We need to develop the extra sense that allows us to hear God's voice in the gentle whispers of the afternoon breeze.

To hear His voice you must be willing to change and obey His words. To achieve the necessary frame of mind and heart, we must recognize that God is good and that He calls us to what is best. His challenge to change is much more than just that. His challenge to change is really a call to growth and to fulfillment. Fulfillment for a person is not a place, it is not a destination, it is a path. Journeying along the path is fulfilling.

Standing still on the path is depressing. When you stand still, you reject "the struggle" and you refuse to change and grow. Simultaneously you reject fulfillment, happiness, the dance for joy, and everything else that is eternally good.

.

may 30

_____

THE CONSTANT temptation is to think if we flipped the list and made number five, work, our new number one, we would get more done. It's a lie. It's a deception. We might for a day, or a week, or even a month or a quarter, but for any meaningful period of time it is not sustainable. Work all night and see how long it takes before the extra work you got done is lost to downtime, fatigue, or lack of focus. The most efficient people I know, those who consistently get the most done, know how to feed the different areas of their lives, and they don't mortgage their higher priorities for their lower priorities . . .

Do you have a value structure? What are your priorities? Let's face it, life is all about choices. We are constantly making choices, but what are we basing our choices on?

We all need some unchanging values and principles to guide us. We live in a world of rapid and continuous change. Such change can be disorienting. The only way to thrive in an environment of change is to know which values are non-negotiable for you.

may 31

IN THIS WORLD that is always racing, we must learn to slow down. We should learn to take control of—and maintain—the rhythm of our own lives. I have always enjoyed walking. To me, it is a time to think about whatever is happening in my life. Recently, I have been trying to walk like a man who doesn't have a worry or care in the world. I begin walking as I have for years now, normally quite quickly, with thoughts chasing through my mind one after the other. As each issue arises, I focus on it and decide whether or not I have done everything within my power regarding the matter. If I discover that I have, I surrender the situation. If I decide that I have not done everything that I should, I resolve to do so and then surrender the situation. I then move on to the next issue and do the same with all the major issues in my life that day.

As the time I spend walking passes, I feel the burden of these various issues lifting from my shoulders, and I find myself slowing down to a nice, steady, peaceful pace. In that rhythm I find a peaceful heart, quiet mind, and restful spirit. Learn to walk like a person who doesn't have a care in the world.

june

june 1

EVERY DAY we are tempted in dozens of ways to have a casual relationship with truth. Many situations emerge each week in which we are tempted to ignore the truth, or bend it, stretch it, or massage it, out of political correctness, a desire to be liked, expediency, or convenience.

But Jesus didn't have a casual relationship with truth, and that is radical. He was interested in getting to the root of things. Through this lens of truth Jesus places everything in its proper place, bringing order to every aspect of life, and demonstrates the true value of things. We all yearn for this divine ordering. The challenge is to surrender and allow God to put our lives in order. The fruit of this surrender is the peace and joy that we all desire.

Jesus was a radical. He reminds us at every turn that God's ways are not a slight variation of man's ways, but that they are in fact radically different. Embrace any one of Jesus' teachings seriously and some of the people around you are bound to think that you are taking it a little too far. His teachings don't invite us to the mediocre middle. They invite us to a radical love.

June 2

LIFE IS MESSY and we are called to put ourselves in the middle of the mess and work to make a difference, however small. We are all carrying a heavy load, fighting a hard battle, but so is every person we encounter in this mystery we call life. Jesus invites us to "take up [our] cross daily" (Matthew 16:24). And some days we are called to take up someone else's cross also, so he can catch his breath, have a short rest, or simply have his faith in the goodness of humanity restored.

Life is messy, and it is not enough just to talk about the mess. We are each called to do something about it. It's time to confront our own mess, how it affects us, and how our mess affects others. But it is also time to reach out to others who have a mess greater or smaller than our own and be with them in their mess.

June 3

_____

THE SCRIPTURES are full of references to the Eucharist, but many people find the leap from these words to the reality of the true presence too daunting. Nonetheless, if you have doubts or disbelief, set them aside for a moment. Suspend your judgment, and imagine it is real. Imagine you could receive the body and blood of Jesus Christ under the guise of bread and wine. Imagine the Catholic experience of the Eucharist is what Jesus had in mind. Imagine how that might transform you. Imagine how receiving the Eucharist might empower you to become more perfectly the person God created you to be. Imagine how that realization would allow you to go out into the world and set it on fire. Imagine if each time we received Jesus in the Eucharist we became a little bit more of whom and what we received. Imagine . . .

There is power in the Eucharist. It is Jesus who walked the earth as our teacher—the same Jesus who died, rose from the dead, and ascended into heaven as our Savior. It is the glorified Jesus who transcends time and space. He is the healer of my soul . . . and he yearns to be the healer of yours.

june 4

ONE OF THE GREATEST gifts my parents ever gave me was the spirit of service. To live an others-centered life is certainly something that is countercultural at a time where young people are actively encouraged to go out and get whatever it is they want for themselves from life. Somewhere, somehow, we have been convinced that living an others-centered life is not going to bring happiness to us. Nothing could be further from the truth.

The happiest people I know are those who have dedicated themselves to a life of service, whether as a parent, as a schoolteacher, in political office, as a minister, in the army, or as a nurse. In the same way, the times when I have been happiest in my life have been those times when I have dedicated myself to helping others in whatever small ways I have been able to do so. Service animates the human spirit. It makes a person shine. Reminds us of our innate power to make a difference. Service affirms the dignity of a person and causes our spirits to soar. The happiest people I know are making a contribution.

June 5

HAVE YOU EVER wondered what God looks for on a resumé? What I mean is, when God is looking for someone to send out on a great mission, what qualities do you think he looks for in that person? I am sure we could each come up with a list of qualities and have a long discussion about which are most important. But then if you compared your list to the types of people God has used to do amazing things throughout history, it probably wouldn't hold up.

God baffles us with his choices. The list of people he has chosen for great mission doesn't hold up to any type of human logic. He almost never chooses the people you and I would choose. The more you delve into it, the more fascinating it becomes. He almost never chooses people in positions of authority, wealth, or power, and he almost never chooses the best educated or the most qualified. What criteria does he use? Just one: God uses those who make themselves available to him. All he asks is that you make yourself available.

june 6

_____

GOD YEARS to be with us. When I am at the office I can't wait to get home and roll around on the floor with my son, to kiss and cuddle him. When I am traveling away from home, I miss my son. I miss his touch, his noises, and the sweet smell of his skin. I yearn to be with him. In the same way, as I reflect on human history and our Judeo-Christian story, what strikes me is the way that God is constantly reaching out to us. God wants to be with us. God yearns to be with us. And so often we complicate our relationship with God when more than anything else, before all the doctrines and after all the dogmas, it would seem that God simply wants to be with us.

june 7

___

ANOTHER OF THE great secrets that we often overlook is that failure is a part of all great achievement and discovery. We live in a culture obsessed with success, and as a result we unconsciously foster the attitude that it is not okay to fail. If you fail, you aren't a failure.

I think baseball teaches us more about failure than any other sport does. A great hitter has a batting average of perhaps .350. What does that tell us? It tells us that he succeeds in hitting the ball only 35 percent of the time. What else does it tell us? It tells us that he fails 65 percent of the time. Francis T. Vincent Jr., while commissioner of baseball, made these observations in a speech at Fairfield University: Baseball teaches us, or has taught most of us, how to deal with failure. We learn at a very young age that failure is the norm in baseball and, precisely because we have failed, we hold in high regard those who fail less often—those who hit safely in one out of three chances and become star players. I also find it fascinating that baseball, alone in sport, considers errors to be a part of the game, part of its rigorous truth. We must never allow our spirit to be stifled by failure. Failure is a part of progress, not a final outcome.

june 8

_____

GOD IS constantly inviting us to grow, to develop, to change, to love more deeply, and to become the whole person he created us to be. This requires a daily conversion of the heart. Begin each day in prayer. Make this a sacred appointment on your calendar. And begin each time of prayer by renewing your availability to God. Never miss your daily prayer time. If something comes up, move it forward; never put your prayer off. If you do, you will almost inevitably find yourself at the end of the day having been busy with so many things that mean so little in the grand scheme of things, but not having spent time with God in this powerful and personal way. Make a promise to yourself and to the one who gave you the very breath that animates your being.

If we cannot set aside these few minutes to spend exclusively with God each day, we will not make ourselves available to him throughout the day. If we do not make ourselves available to him entirely for the promised time, it will be too easy to exclude him from the other parts of our days and lives. Make a promise and keep that promise, one day at a time.

june 9

IT SEEMS TO ME we should never think deeply about anything without first considering the purpose of that thing. The purpose of culture is to help an organization better fulfill its mission with the understanding that a healthy environment will best serve that mission in the long run. From that perspective, culture is everything an organization does that helps it become the-very-best-version-of-itself, and everything it does to fulfill its mission better this year than it did last year.

It is very important to remember this single outrageous idea when we are discussing culture: We are here to work. I know it may seem like a blatant announcement of the obvious, but too often that reality gets thrown out the window when organizations start talking about culture. When we forget we are here to work, when we disconnect our discussions about culture from our individual work and collective mission, those conversations move quickly toward things that can actually be a real distraction from the work at hand. I know it may seem crazy, but when it comes to work, we are actually here to accomplish something.

june 10

_____

CONSIDER THIS. Two patient people will always have a better relationship than two impatient people. Two generous people will always have a better relationship than two selfish people. Two courageous people will always have a better relationship than two cowardly people. Two humble people will always have a better relationship than two prideful people. And every aspect of society—in a family, among a community, within an organization, or even between nations—is an extension and multiplication of this single relationship.

Think of it in this way. Who would you prefer as your employees or colleagues: men and women of virtue or those riddled with vice and selfishness? Would you prefer your neighbors be patient or impatient? Would you rather your extended family be generous or self-seeking? Would you prefer honest or dishonest customers? Would you rather have a courageous or a cowardly manager?

The whole world prefers virtue.

june 11

WILL I BE ABLE to instruct my son adequately about the beauty and genius of Catholicism? Will the Church learn to speak directly to the triumphs and trials, the questions and concerns of his life? I hope so.

If I could teach my son one thing that would ensure his appreciation of Catholicism, what would it be?

When I receive the Eucharist it's a pivotal moment in my week. It's a moment of transformation, a moment where I get to receive who and what I wish to become. And I cannot leave that. It wouldn't matter how good the music or preaching was elsewhere, I cannot leave the Eucharist. I cannot leave Jesus.

And so, sitting there with my son, I discovered that one thing I could teach him to ensure his appreciation of Catholicism: I could teach my son to appreciate the true presence of Jesus in the Eucharist. For it is the belief that Jesus is truly present in the Eucharist—not just symbolically so—that seems to be one of the key differences between highly engaged Catholics and those who walk away from the Church. It may be the difference.

june 12

———————————

A MAN'S TRUE SELF lies within his values, principles, morals, and ethics. He can't be his true self if you take him away from these things. If you do take him away from them, you can be certain of one thing: sooner or later, he will leave you to get back to his true self.

He will leave you to get back to his morals, ethics, principles, and values, because he can't live without them. Not happily. He will never have peace if he is separated from them, and the human spirit yearns for that peace. Our lives are a constant searching for that peace. It is the peace of being aligned with our true selves. It is the peace that all men seek, but that a rare few ever find.

Yes, we all like to experience the pleasures of this world. Certainly, one person enjoys pleasure as much as the next. But while we can live without pleasure, we can't live without our true self . . . and we can only find our true self in and through morals, values, principles, and the ethical way of life.

june 13

DO YOU EVER feel you just need a little time to yourself? Do you find yourself questioning the way you are living your life? Do you have questions about what is best for you now? Do you feel overloaded or overwhelmed?

All of these are signs that you need a little silence, solitude, and simplicity. These feelings and questions are our spiritual desires trying desperately to be heard.

June 14

_____

WITHIN EACH and every single one of us lies something of greater beauty than anything our eyes have ever rested on.

Within each of us there is a flower wanting to bloom. The flower within you that wants to bloom is your soul. The Divine Gardener wishes to work the ground. The Divine Gardener wishes to water the ground. He wishes to pull out the weeds and place the flower where it can get just the right amount of sunlight.

Listen to the voice of the Divine Gardener. Remember, when He points out your faults and failings, He is hoeing the earth of your soul and pulling out the weeds. Some parts of the gardening process are painful, but the pain gives birth to new life. Allow Him to direct you, to call you forth, to move you, remembering that He wants to place you where you will get just the right amount of sunlight.

Listen. Listen. Listen.

june 15

GOD IS HAPPY. In fact, God is Happiness. Our happiness is dependent on whether or not we actively take steps to unite ourselves with God. Sin separates us from God and makes us unhappy. When will we wake up and see that sin is self-destructive? Sin doesn't make God unhappy, it makes us unhappy. Our task is to become one with God. The attainment of everything good that we desire for ourselves, our neighbor, and our world is dependent on us becoming one with God. We become one with God by raising our hearts and minds to truth, goodness, and the things of the spirit. We become one with God through prayer and the sacraments. It is through prayer, the sacraments, and indeed any spiritual activity that we learn to walk with God. When we walk with Him, we learn His ways, His wisdom, His love, and His boundless joy. The path of salvation is an exciting journey; it is one designed for our own good, but often it is not portrayed or understood in this light.

june 16

ALWAYS TAKE your first opportunity each day to spend time in prayer. The daily habit of prayer leads us to spiritual health. The more ingrained this habit becomes in our lives, the clearer we hear the voice of God. The clearer we hear the voice of God in our lives, the more likely we are to walk in his ways, honor his will, and experience the peace and happiness he yearns to fill us with.

june 17

THE SIOUX BELIEVED that the longest journey we can make in this life is from the head to the heart. This is also the longest spiritual journey we can make; it is the pilgrimage of prayer. We think of the heart as emotional, and it is, but it is also deeply spiritual. Are you living your life from the mind? Are you living your life from the heart? Or have you found the delicate balance between the heart and the mind that allows you to live in growing wisdom? Prayer helps us make the journey from the head to the heart, and it is prayer that allows us to balance the heart and mind so that we can live in wisdom.

Every journey has a series of ordinary moments, but there are other moments that stand out as significant. The significant moments on the pilgrimage of our lives usually present us with a choice that needs to be made. There is a great spiritual decision before you right now: To make prayer a daily habit in your life or not? This is a choice that will affect you every day for the rest of your life.

june 18

IF YOU CAME TO ME and told me that you wanted to become a great basketball player, I would tell you to study the great players who have gone before you. Learn everything you can about Michael Jordan, Larry Bird, and Magic Johnson. Read books, watch videos, research their training techniques—find out what qualities led them to become extraordinary athletes. If you want to be a great artist, study other great artists. If you want to be a great business leader, study other great business leaders. And of course this same principle applies to those of us who want to become great Catholics. Whom will you study? There is a path that leads to the authentic life. It is not a secret path; the path to holiness is well worn. For two thousand years, men and women of all ages, from all walks of life and every social class, have been treading this path. If you came to me and told me you were going on a journey to a place you had never been before, I would advise you to travel with a guide. If you had to choose a guide, you wouldn't choose someone who had never been to where you wanted to go. You would choose an expert, someone who has made the journey before.

june 19

EXERCISE IS SOULFUL. Eating foods that fuel and energize the body is soulful. When we take care of ourselves physically, we live soulfully. Emotional vitality is a sign of soulfulness. Soulful people have intellectual curiosity. Tending to our souls, exploring the life of the spirit, is soulful living. Soulful living animates the human person—it brings us to life—and soulful living is achieved by connecting the seemingly trivial activities of our everyday lives with our essential purpose. Washing the car is just washing the car, until you decide to do it to the best of your ability because doing so will help you become the-best-version-of-yourself. Cooking dinner for your family is just cooking dinner for your family, until you decide to do it to the best of your ability and to make a meal that will help you all become the-best-version-of-yourselves. Even the most trivial activities of our lives take on great meaning when we approach them with our essential purpose in mind. Living soulfully means doing everything with your essential purpose in mind. Soulfulness is a way of life, which once tasted becomes an obsession. Soulful people have large and generous hearts. They live in a world of appreciation and abundance and their love of life is contagious.

June 20

_____

THE STORY OF Edison's effort to find a way to keep a light bulb burning is well known. He tried more than ten thousand combinations of materials before he found the one that worked. People asked him later in his life how he could continue after failing that many times. He said he didn't see the other attempts as failures. He then went on to explain that he had successfully identified ten thousand ways that didn't work and that each attempt brought him closer to the one that would. He saw his failures as progress.

Why do we perpetuate the belief that it is not okay to fail? Failure plays an important role in our development and a critical role in our attempts to become perfectly ourselves. Whatever pattern of defeat you may find yourself in right now, remember these three abiding truths:

1. Other people before you have successfully overcome the obstacles you face; seek them out and draw strength from their stories and example.

2. All of your past failures leave you better equipped than ever before to succeed in your next attempt.

3. It will never be easier to break that pattern of defeat than it is right now.

june 21

_____

ONE BY ONE, each day of creation reveals another level of humanity's dependence on the other elements of nature. We are dependent on the sun for light and energy. We are dependent on water. We are dependent on trees for fresh air, on plants and vegetation for food and nourishment . . .

It makes sense that God created us dependent on them, so that we would not abuse and destroy them. Perhaps the idea in the mind of God was, if we were dependent on the other elements of nature, we would respect and live in harmony with them.

From this narrative of creation I wish to draw attention to two themes: our dependency on the other elements of nature and the institution of rest as a divine pastime.

The actions of God so often are a response to the needs of humanity. On the seventh day God rested. God did not need to rest. He did, however, foresee our need for rest.

june 22

———————

HOW OFTEN do we convince ourselves consciously or subconsciously that if we get the car, the dress, the bag, the watch, the job, the guy, the girl, the house, the trip . . . we will be happy? This leads to two outcomes. The first is bad but not as diabolical as the second. The first outcome is we get the car, for example, and for a few days or weeks we are delighted and completely enamored with it. Getting the car has brought some measure of happiness, but that happiness is circumstantial; it is dependent on the car. If the car were taken away, the happiness would evaporate. In fact, we would probably be even unhappier than we were before we ever got the car. That's the first outcome—we get the car, it brings a measure of happiness, and that happiness soon fades.

As I mentioned, the second outcome is even worse. In scenario number two we don't get the car, the job, or the girl, and we spend the rest of our life in a self-imposed victimhood believing that if only we had gotten the car, the job, or the girl, we would have been happy forever. The person who never gets the car never works out that the car was never going to make him really happy. So he lives perpetually in the false promise.

june 23

_____

ONE OF THE many privileges my work has afforded me is the opportunities I have to work with young people, particularly teenagers. The question I have been asking myself for years now is: What do they all have in common? The answer of course is many things, and most people can probably name most of the things these young people have in common. The surprise discovery for me has been their need for an obsession.

As I have reflected on it, I have come to believe we all need an obsession, not just young people. We need it because paradoxically a healthy obsession brings focus and balance to our minds and lives. In addition, obsessions breed passion, energy, enthusiasm, and vitality. It is obsession that gets us out of bed in the morning, and those of us who don't have one find it just that little bit harder to get out of bed with each passing year. What is your obsession?

How do we know which are good and which are bad? Easy enough, those that help us to become a-better-version-of-ourselves are the ones we should pursue and celebrate.

june 24

_____

EVERYONE EVANGELIZES about something, but most of us evangelize about the wrong things. Have you seen how passionate some people are when they talk about their iPhone? They tell you why they love it so much, point out the favorite apps and features, and by the time they are finished you probably want one yourself. That is evangelization. Other people evangelize about their car, their company, or their favorite vacation destination. It's amazing how animated we can become about things that are trivial. It is in our nature to evangelize. Sadly, many people have nothing better than their iPhone or favorite vacation place to evangelize about.

We are all evangelists. What are you evangelizing about?

June 25

DIFFERENT people respond in different ways to the storms in their relationships. Some people run. We are all capable of this type of cowardice, and when someone acts in a cowardly fashion we are rarely able to change his or her mind. Others madly scramble about in an effort to sink roots. This is a natural and noble reaction. Still others pull up the roots that they have spent the years of their relationship sinking. This is madness, but crisis makes many temporarily insane.

What are the roots that will help our relationships weather the inevitable storms? Communication, appreciation, respect, a mutual willingness to serve, annual vacations are just a few. But there are too many to name; the list is endless. As with diets, there are hundreds of them, thousands of them. Which one works? Almost all of them will work for almost all people. Diets don't fail. People fail at diets. We get lazy and neglect the basic resolutions. You may not know what the storm looks like, but you know the storm is coming. Now is the time to prepare.

june 26

———————

THE DAILY HABIT of prayer leads us to recognize God presence in every aspect and moment of our lives. Not that he is in our presence, but that we are continually in his presence. To pray is to live in the presence of God. As we commit ourselves to a daily practice of prayer, our spiritual senses begin to awaken, and we become aware of God at our side throughout the day. The stronger our connection with God, the more easily we recognize his presence in every moment of every day. There are moments in life that are so arresting that even the most spiritually unaware person cannot help but recognize God's presence. The first time a newborn baby smiles, most people are stricken with an awe and a recognition that God is present. It is much harder to recognize God in the pain of a beggar on the street or in the eyes of someone you do not particularly like.

God is with us, in each moment. Always, not sometimes. He didn't want us looking for him in the past or the future. God is not around the corner or over the next hill; he is by our side.

June 27

_____

GOD HAS PLACED you here for some purpose, but without discipline, you will never discover that purpose. Without discipline, you will march slowly and surely to join Thoreau's masses leading "lives of quiet desperation."

Mozart was a great composer, but did he begin as a great composer? No. He began as a keen student, mastering the discipline of playing the harpsichord. Only then, from this mastery and discipline, did the individual style and genius emerge.

Did Picasso find his unique style on his first day at art school? No. First he learned to paint a bowl of fruit like a photograph. Only then, having mastered the discipline of painting, did the individual style and genius that we know today as Picasso emerge.

First discipline, then genius.

june 28

_____

OUR DESIRE to take the path of least resistance can also prevent us from walking the path of truth, happiness, and freedom. We don't want to rock the boat. We don't want our friends to think we are different. We don't want to upset anyone. Are your friends as happy and fulfilled as you want to be?

You don't want your friends to think you are different, but you don't want to be like them. So you have to be different; otherwise you will end up like them. And if ending up like them means being caught up in the things of this world and forming disordered attachments, then you will end up unhappy. If you want to experience a happiness and joy that are radically different from your present state, then you must adopt a radically different lifestyle.

What holds us back? More than anything else, we do. We hold ourselves back from the very things we desire.

june 29

THE GOAL of the Christian life is to live a holy life. Those who have attained this goal we call saints. They found their essential purpose, they pursued their essential purpose, and they celebrated their essential purpose. The saints responded to the universal call to holiness and followed that great spiritual North Star. They quietly chiseled away at the defects and weaknesses in their character. They became the-best-version-of-themselves. They have truly applied themselves to the Christian life. They have brought the Gospel to life, animating it with their own thoughts, words, and actions. They have lived authentic lives. I ask you to consider who has lived more fully than the saints.

june 30

I READ a very powerful line in Richard Foster's work, Celebration of Discipline. In it, he discusses the ways possessions can complicate and rule our lives: "Learn to enjoy things without having to own them." It struck me very deeply, because I like having my own things. But it made me realize that sometimes it is more enjoyable to be able to use something for the day or a week, or even a month, and not have to give it permanent space in your mind.

One of the most powerful ways for us to simplify our lives is in the area of money and things. Examining our attitudes toward money and things can also provide valuable insight into how we perceive ourselves, and the motives that drive us.

july

july 1

YOUR EXPERIENCE of life expands with the more energy you have. Think about that. I don't write these words lightly. Your experience of life is not a small thing. It is not insignificant. We are not talking about what route you take to work or what you will have for lunch. We are talking about the all-encompassing experience of life. So I will say it again. Your experience of life expands with the more energy you have . . .

When were you last overflowing with energy and enthusiasm for life? Has it been a while? Are you tired of being tired? If so, great! But are you fed up enough to do something about it? Experience tells me you won't change until the pain of not changing is greater than the pain of changing. The only exception to that rule is a life-changing experience. It could be an event. A friend of mine lost his father to cancer, his brother in a car accident, and his best friend to depression and suicide all in two years. The following year he made some radical changes to the way he was living. The life-changing experience could be a seminar, a book, or a new friend. The important thing to realize is that we can change our lives—and change them significantly.

july 2

NOW IMAGINE if Jesus owned an airline. The pre-boarding announcement would be: "Ladies and gentleman, welcome to Jesus Air. We do things differently here. We are delighted that you are joining us and we are looking forward to serving you so that you can have an incredible experience. At Jesus Air we board by zones. Zone 1 consists of those with absolutely no status in this world, the lowest of the low on the frequent-flyer totem pole. Zone 2 consists of our Silver members. Zone 3 is for our Gold members. Zone 4 will consist of our Platinum members. And finally Zone 5, in which there are only middle seats left and absolutely no overhead space for your carry-ons, is for those overprivileged, constantly pampered Diamond members. At Jesus Air our motto is the first shall be last and the last shall be first. Thank you for flying Jesus Air."

We all enjoy VIP service, but Jesus tells us that the least among us deserve it too. Who are the least among you? How are you treating them? Jesus tells us that we should be giving them preferential treatment. Sobering, isn't it? Radical.

july 3

IS FREEDOM, then, the core of the human experience we call life? No. Love is the essence of life. Love is life's great joy and her greatest lesson. Love is the one task worthy of life. We busy ourselves with so many things, while the one great task we set aside, ignore, neglect. Love is your task—to love yourself by striving to becoming the-best-version-of-yourself, to love others by encouraging them and assisting them in their quest to become the-best-versions-of-themselves, and to love God by becoming all you were created to be.

But in order to love, you must be free, for to love is to give your self to someone or something freely, completely, unconditionally, and without reservation. It is as if you could take the essence of your very self in your hands and give it to another person. Yet to give your self—to another person, to an endeavor, or to God—you must first possess your self. This possession of self is freedom. It is a prerequisite for love, and is attained only through discipline.

july 4

DO YOU NEED REFORM? What part of your life most needs it? From time to time, everything and everyone needs a good reformation. How's your marriage? How are your personal finances? How is your physical fitness? How's your spiritual health? How is your work/career? Family life? Sooner or later, under the weight of our collective complacency most things fall into mediocrity and become something very different than they were intended to be. The next question is, are you willing to make the sacrifices necessary to bring about reform? The thing about Saint Bernard is he was prepared to lay down his life for reform, to make something better.

Reform, renewal, transformation, and change—these are beautiful things when they lead to something that is renewed, refreshed, and improved . . . Whatever you sense needs reformation in your life, God years to collaborate with you in that reformation Do not be afraid. Be bold. Live boldly even if you are surrounded by cowards and critics.

july 5

AS HUMAN BEINGS, we get mesmerized by shiny things. It happens in relationships and careers, and it happens to organizations. They make the effort and spend the time to put together a solid Strategic Plan, but then they get distracted and mesmerized by shiny things.

Don't let that happen. The irresistible opportunity is the success trap. To stay focused and disciplined, sometimes you need to resist the irresistible. The problem is, people and organizations spend their whole lives trying to become successful and looking for great opportunities. Once you get a little bit successful, suddenly the ideas and opportunities come looking for you. Now there are more ideas and opportunities than could possibly be pursued. And the more successful you become, the more really good ideas and opportunities come your way. That's the problem. The success trap is too many good opportunities. All of those opportunities are a distraction. Focus on the plan.

july 6

_____

TOWARD THE END of his life, he used to recall in interviews: "When I was a child, my mother used to say to me over and over again, 'Pablo, if you become a soldier you will be a general and if you become a priest you will be Pope.' But I became an artist, and so, I became Picasso."

Each and every one of us must make this same journey from the expectations of others to the celebration of the true self God created us to be. To become who you were created to be is the only thing that matters and is the only true and lasting success. The great challenge is not to succeed in the world's eyes, but rather to discover what your unique abilities are and offer them to the world in the best way you can. To feel at home with who you are and where you are and what you are doing is worth more than all the treasures and pleasures money can buy. The real challenge is not the quest for success but the quest to create inner peace by being faithful to who we truly are, created wonderfully and uniquely by God.

july 7

MANY YEARS AGO I wrote: "People don't do anything until they are inspired, but once they are inspired there is almost nothing they won't do." I believed it then and I believe it now. I have seen it time and time again. Inspiration sets free our pent-up possibilities, filling us with the boldness to live life to the fullest. There are many ways to be inspired. Music is inspiring. Nature is inspiring. A great speech is inspiring. The birth of a child is inspiring. A well-lived life is inspiring. Parents working hard to support their family inspires me. Smile lines in an old woman's face are beautiful and inspiring. Traveling to different places and meeting different people is inspiring. Movies inspire me. Books inspire me. There are so many ways to be inspired, and for me, well, I guess I've noticed over the years that I need a little inspiration every day.

july 8

HOW DO WE condition ourselves to desire the things that are best for us? We desire the things we ponder. We desire the things we see every day. Television is a perfect example. The combined audiovisual stimulus impacts us powerfully. We respond to the on-screen images with desire. What happens when you see something you like on television? You want it. In her book, The Overspent American, Juliet Schor describes a survey she conducted in 1998. Ms. Schor's research revealed that for every hour of television watched weekly, the consumer's spending rose by $208 a year.

We desire the things we ponder, the things we hold in our mind, and as such television is a form of pondering. Television drives consumer aspirations, not just through the commercials, but through the stylish clothing worn by actors and the affluent settings of many of the shows. Great sporting champions ponder and desire victory. Great entrepreneurs ponder and desire financial wealth. Great saints ponder and desire intimacy with God. If you begin to ponder the things that are good for you, you will begin to desire them. If you begin to desire them, you will soon begin to attain them.

july 9

WHETHER YOU are struggling to overcome a pattern of defeat, yearning for inner peace, trying to create lasting happiness, wishing to succeed in your career, desperately trying to overcome procrastination, or battling with an addiction, this lesson holds the key for you. Just do the next right thing. In each moment, just keep doing the next right thing. Whenever you get into a funk, just do the next right thing. And keep doing the next right thing. You will be amazed at how quickly you work yourself out of the funk if you approach it in this way. Don't worry about next week or next month or next year. Just do the next right thing and keep doing the next right thing, and gradually you will act your way out of destructive patterns. You cannot think or pray or wish or hope yourself out of the pattern that is holding you back. You must act your way out of it, one moment at a time.

One moment at a time, by simply doing the next right thing, you will move from confusion to clarity, from misunderstanding to insight, from despair to hope, from darkness to light, and discover your truest self, the unique person God designed you to be.

july 10

WHEN YOU ACKNOWLEDGE your imperfections, you are on the brink of great growth and wonderful times. None of us is perfect. We have all witnessed ourselves and others failing in different areas of our lives. Some allow their failure to be transformed into despair and defeat. Others are able to get up, move on, and struggle again. Some failures just look like failures. Other failures really are failures and need to be recognized as such.

Vincent Van Gogh, the Dutch painter, is now hailed as one of the greatest artists of all time. But he did not enjoy the same acclaim and success during his lifetime. He painted 1,700 paintings; during his lifetime he sold only one of them, for a mere eighty-five dollars. Almost one hundred years to the day after his death, one of his paintings was sold at action for forty million dollars. Some failures just look like failures.

Imagine if after painting five pictures and not being able to sell them, Van Gogh had quit. Today we would not have Sunflowers and so many of his other works to enjoy.

july 11

_____

GRATITUDE CHANGES our lives. It changes the way we feel about ourselves, the way we feel about life, and the way we feel about others. If we can summon the courage to speak our gratitude to others it will give them the encouragement they need to keep striving to become the-best-version-of-themselves. I have found that both children and adults beam when we catch them doing something right and praise them.

There are 6 billion people on the planet and I suspect that 5.9 billion of them go to bed every night starving for one honest word of appreciation. Learn to appreciate and praise those you love. We all need encouragement. Becoming the-best-version-of-ourselves can be a daunting task! Commit to complimenting your significant other for something you appreciate about him or her at least once a week. Make gratitude one of the roots that allow your relationship to grow strong.

july 12

"PRAY CONSTANTLY" was St. Paul's invitation, and it is a beautiful principle of the spiritual life. But if most have not been taught how to pray and establish a habit of daily prayer in their lives, you can be certain they have not been taught how to transform the ordinary moments of their days into prayer. Every honest human activity can be transformed into prayer. Learning to transform daily activities into prayer was one of the greatest spiritual lessons of my life. And it is so simple. Offer the next hour of your work for a friend who is sick. Offer the task you are least looking forward to today to God as a prayer for the person you know who is suffering most today, and do that task with great love, better than you have ever done it. Offer each task, one at a time, to God as a prayer for a specific intention, and do so with love. Pray for others as they come to mind throughout the day. This is how we are able to keep the epic conversation going, this never-ending conversation between you and God—by acknowledging him in the activities and affairs of our lives. Prayer is the conversation of a lifetime, and a lifetime of conversation. It's ongoing and constant. And what is more important than this conversation?

july 13

GOD LOVES US. We hear this all the time in Christian circles, and for some reason I have always believed it. But now I feel it. It has become real to me in fatherhood. You see, I love my son so much. I love him more than I ever thought I was capable of loving. And if I can love him this much—with all my weakness, brokenness, and limitations—how much God must love his children.

july 14

PEOPLE ARE ALWAYS asking me three questions: What sort of books do you read? Who inspires you? Who are your heroes and role models? Most people are then surprised to hear that I don't read much. I love to read, but I am in fact a very slow reader. I rarely read for entertainment. I read to expand my vision of the world, myself, and God, with the hope that it will make me a better person. And while I do not read for hours at a time, I do read the Gospels every day. These four books are the foundation upon which I try to base my life more and more with each passing day. And so every day, even if only for ten minutes, I read from one of these great spiritual touchstones. Apart from the Gospels, I am usually in the midst of a good spiritual book, a novel of some type, a biography, and a business book.

july 15

_____

WHEN WE TAKE time to reflect on the beauty of nature, the extraordinary wonder of the human being, and the great mystery that we possess the ability to both love and be loved, our natural response is reverence. From this reverence is born the respect that is an indispensable ingredient of all successful relationships.

To respect is to value people and things in their proper order. Respect is one of the great cornerstones of relationships. Respect fosters trust and encourages openness and honesty. We should show respect for other people even before they have done anything to deserve it, simply because they are human beings. Respect re-minds people of their innate and extraordinary value even if they have forgotten it themselves. At the same time, we should always expect to have to earn the respect of others.

july 16

FOR THE DAY we accept that we have chosen to choose our choices is the day we cast off the shackles of victimhood and are set free to pursue the lives we were born to live.

Learn to master the moment of decision and you will live a life uncommon.

july 17

_____

ONE OF THE MOST incredible abilities God has given the human person is the ability to dream. We are able to look into the future and imagine something better than today, and then return to the present and work to make that richly imagined future a reality.

july 18

WE READ IN Proverbs 29:18, "Where there is no vision, the people will perish." In a land where there are no musicians; in a land where there are no storytellers, teachers, or poets; in a land where there are no men and women of vision and leadership; in a land where there are no legends, saints, or champions; in a land where there are no dreamers—the people of that land will most certainly perish.

But you and I, we are the music makers; we are the storytellers, teachers, and poets; we are the men and women of vision and leadership; we are the legends, the saints, and the champions; and we are the dreamers of the dreams.

july 19

IMAGE OR LIGHT, that is the question. We tend to spend our lives dedicated to the image, to the material. The image represents the body. The light represents the spirit. Do you identify more with your body or with your spirit? The highest levels of living are experienced when we have an absolute disregard for the body beyond our basic needs and a complete adherence to the promptings of the Divine Spirit within us. It is then that we form our identity from the spirit within, when we let the sweet light within us shine.

Most of us, however, are dedicated to the body, to the image. We see and value ourselves not in terms of the spirit, but in relation to the body. We find our identity through the body. We form, and live by, an image made up of physical and sensory perception.

Do you find your identity through your body or through your spirit? Are you dedicated to the image or to the light? The image is an illusion. The light is truth.

A person who is completely dedicated to the light is capable of anything. Prayer shifts our dedication from the image to the light.

july 20

YOU CAN HAVE a more satisfying life. You can have both personal and professional satisfaction. But nobody is going to just give it to you. It must be sought with relentless desire and commitment. Above all else, satisfaction must be sought patiently and with an overwhelming sense that we are responsible for creating satisfaction. While we can contribute to the satisfaction of others, nobody can be wholly responsible for our satisfaction other than ourselves.

Does this scare you? I hope it does. If it does not, I fear you have skipped over the words without fully recognizing their truth. So let me say it this way. If you have a life filled with satisfaction, very good, you have given yourself this gift. If you have a life that lacks satisfaction, it is so, but only because you have chosen it. But you can choose again . . . beginning today, beginning now. Lillian Hellman wrote, "It's a sad day when you find out that it's not accident or time or fortune, but just yourself that kept things from you." I disagree. I think it is a happy day, as long as you are willing to do something about it. Are you willing to do something about the dissatisfaction in your life?

july 21

THE WORLD NEEDS changing, and the truth is, it will not likely change for the better unless this change is led by Christians. No group of people is in a better position to change the world than Christians, but we need to get our act together; we need to get organized, unified, and mobilized.

What is it that the world needs? Holy Moments.

Your marriage needs Holy Moments. This is what your children, friends, neighbors, and work colleagues need. Your school, business, and church all need Holy Moments.

This simple and beautiful idea is central to the Christian life, despite the fact that we have lost sight of it or abandoned it, or both. It is accessible to all men, women, and children, and it doesn't require a towering intellect. Rich and poor, educated and uneducated, single and married—everyone can understand this uncomplicated approach to transforming the simple moments of our everyday lives into moments that transform us and other people and bring about a better world where our children and grandchildren can grow free and strong.

july 22

FRIENDSHIP IS the most natural and effective way to share the faith with others. If we are friends and I say something that you disagree with, you are not likely to dismiss it without consideration. Out of the respect that is built through the course of a friendship, you will consider my point of view, even if you disagree with it. Inviting people to explore their questions of faith in a new way is asking them to rethink the way they live their lives—often in major ways. It is the respect that is born through friendship that allows people to let their guard down and consider a new way.

Christian friendship is not just about common interests; it is about helping each other become the-best-version-of-ourselves. A friendship that places the other person's best interests above our own selfish desires or agenda is quite rare in this world. Often when people first experience this kind of friendship they don't believe it. Christian friendship seems too good to be true in the current cultural landscape. And so it takes time to convince people that our friendship is genuine and rightly motivated. But it is this type of friendship that becomes the vehicle for the faith to spread.

july 23

IF YOU WERE having lunch with God, would you leave to attend to some other matter? If you were on the phone with God, who or what would be important enough that you would put him on hold? Everything is trivial compared to God, and even the most mundane task becomes abundantly meaningful when we include God. And when we include him, the mere knowledge of his presence leads us to seek out behaviors, people, and experiences that are good for us and avoid those that are not.

Guide God around your life. "Lord, we are going to have lunch with my friend Anthony today. He has had a hard time in his marriage lately; please encourage him." In this way, your whole life becomes a prayer, an epic conversation with God. This constant litany of prayers for the people in your life, calling God's grace and mercy upon all who cross your path is truly an elevated way of living. The more we engage in this epic conversation the more powerful our connection with God becomes, and the more we become his ambassadors of peace and love in the world.

july 24

———————

THERE ARE HUNDREDS of examples of men and women who have persisted despite failure or apparent failure. Another of these is Babe Ruth, one of the greatest baseball players of all time. Babe Ruth knew one thing: he could hit a baseball out of the park. He did what he knew, and he did it often—a total of 714 times. But Babe Ruth had his share of failures too. He had to walk back to the dugout 1,330 times after striking out in front of thousands of people. Imagine if after Babe Ruth had struck out one hundred times he had said to himself, "Well, one hundred times is enough times to make any mistake. I quit." And yet so often we quit long before we have even reached one hundred.

How do you respond to failure? When you fail, particularly in your struggle to become a better person, how do you respond?

july 25

CLUTTER, congestion, and confusion have become an accepted part of most people's everyday experience of life, but it doesn't need to be that way. We have chosen and created the clutter and congestion. As hard as it may be to get our minds around at first, by creating the clutter and confusion we have created the confusion in our hearts, minds, and lives. But once we can bring ourselves to realize that we have chosen and created the clutter, congestion, and confusion of our lives, we are free to choose to be rid of it. Admitting that we had a role in the creation of a situation frees us from victimhood and empowers us to play a role in its recreation.

The time has come to recreate. "You are worried and distracted by so many things," was Jesus' observation; "but only one thing is necessary" (Luke 10:41–42) was his advice. Allow these three words to permeate every corner of your being and every aspect of your life, and you will live a life of such authenticity that has rarely been witnessed. Simplify. Simplify. Simplify. Simplicity is the way to clarity.

july 26

COLLABORATION suggests that we are all rowing in the same direction. So, once you have determined who your collaborators are, you need to communicate your vision to them. Tell your child's teachers and coaches: "I want to do everything I can to encourage my child to become the-best-version-of-herself. This is the language I use to communicate with her. It would be great if you could reinforce this idea with this language." What you will discover is that most people don't have a vision, and if your vision is compelling, they will gladly support you in it, and, even better, they will adopt it as their own. Before long, the teacher or coach will be encouraging all his students to become the-best-version-of-themselves.

Great leaders know they cannot do everything on their own, and they expand their influence by choosing great partners to collaborate with.

july 27

MORE THAN twenty years ago, I developed the habit of stopping by church for a few minutes each day to sit with Jesus, present in the tabernacle, and talk about what was happening in my life. The clarity that has emerged from these conversations with Christ in the Eucharist is undeniable. Over the years I have slipped in and out of this habit. Like most people I have told myself that I can pray anywhere, but it just isn't the same. There is something powerful about his presence in the tabernacle.

Years ago, I wrote, "All the answers are in the tabernacle." With every passing year I believe this more intensely.

If you have never done it, stop by your church for ten minutes every day for two weeks. Sit as close to the tabernacle as you can. Speak to Jesus about whatever is on your mind. Or just sit there with him. After two weeks, tell me if you are not a better-version-of-yourself. I believe you will find that you are more patient and joyful, more considerate and compassionate—more human. And to be more human is a beautiful thing.

july 28

MOST PEOPLE in relationships are making promises they cannot keep. They are promising to give themselves in ways they are simply not able to, because they do not possess themselves. They have no self-mastery and therefore they are not free. To love, we must be free. Only to the extent that we are able to wrench ourselves away from the slavery of temper, appetites, and impulses will we be able to love and be loved. This is why there is such a poverty of love and dynamic relationships in our culture, because for those addicted to instant gratification, a lasting relationship is an impossible dream.

I like nice things and wonderful food and spontaneous living as much as the next person. I am not proposing that we give up all the wonderful pleasures of this world, just that we temper our approach to them so that we can more fully savor them as we taste and experience them. It is time we sought freedom from the tyrants within that tie us up and tie us down, that stop us from flying and becoming perfectly ourselves. Discipline makes us free.

july 29

MANY YEARS AGO, I walked the Camino, the old road to Santiago de Compostela. In preparing, I had studied the route and researched what to take with me. The guidebooks were emphatic that you should not take more than twenty pounds of provisions in your backpack. At first, I thought this impossible. How was I to survive for almost a month with so little? I stuffed that backpack till it was brimming with stuff.

At the end of the first day, I left a couple of things behind in the hostel for another pilgrim who might need them. The same happened over the next several days until, by day six, I had reduced what I'd thought I would need to what I actually needed. But as the journey went on, I found I needed less and less. By the time I arrived in Santiago, my backpack was slack and more than half-empty.

We need so little, but we burden ourselves with so much. And every unnecessary thing we burden ourselves with creates an obstacle between us and God. It is also a lesson that you don't need to travel to the other side of the world to learn.

july 30

HISTORY IS FULL of examples of men and women who have become all they were created to be—we call them saints. Some of them were priests, monks, or nuns. Some were married and others were single. Some were rich; others were poor. Some were educated; others were uneducated. Some were young and some were old. Holiness is for everyone— no exceptions. Holiness is for you. Every day God invites you to be all he created you to be.

Holiness brings us to life. It refines every human ability. Holiness doesn't dampen our emotions; it elevates them. Those who respond to God's call to holiness are the most joyful people in history. They have a richer, more abundant experience of life, and they love more deeply than most people can ever imagine. They enjoy life, all of life. Even in the midst of suffering they are able to maintain a peace and a joy that are independent of the happenings and circumstances surrounding them. Holiness doesn't stifle us; it sets us free.

july 31

IN A CULTURE obsessed with the value of time, one of the real and tangible ways for us to let people know that we care, that we are interested in trying to know them, is to give them our time. Not grudgingly and stingily, but lavishly. Love is generous and abundant. By lavishing our time upon the people we love, we demonstrate that we love them, that we care about them, and that we are willing to make an effort to know and be known.

Carefree timelessness is the key to moving beyond the first level of intimacy, out of the impersonal world of clichés and into the world of personal conversation. In fact, the lesson of carefree timelessness plays a significant role in all seven levels of intimacy. Give the gift of carefree timelessness to your significant other, to your children, to your parents, to everyone with whom you have a high-level relationship. Give the people you love the gift of carefree timelessness. It will transform them, and you, and the relationships you share. Then and only then, restored once more by that carefree timelessness, together, will you discover the lightheartedness essential to the thriving we were given this life to enjoy.

august

august 1

_____

WHAT I DELIGHT in most about St. Francis is that the people who loved him honored him by remembering his story—all of his story, even his wild youth and his moments of impatience during the early days of his ministry. It is for this reason that biographers have been so successful at portraying Francis as a "whole man" rather than as a caricature of holiness. He was certainly saintly, but not sanctimonious. He loved God, but he also loved his neighbor and creation.

Francis was real. He was striving with all his heart to live an authentic life. And like the first Christians, he captured the imaginations and intrigued the hearts and minds of the people of his time and the people of times to come. Francis is a practical example of the power of one authentic life indelibly engraved upon history.

august 2

CRYSTALLIZE your purpose. Work out what your life principle is going to be. Write it down in your own words . . .

Remind yourself of your goal in every waking moment of every hour of every day—that's what successful people do. They dream the dream, define the dream, continually visualize the dream—and they achieve the dream.

Then live it. Allow your life principle to become the foundation of all activity in your life. Let it become your guide and adviser in times of decision, let it become your comforter and assurance in times of fear and doubt. Allow it to affect every decision and action of your day. Allow it to become your life principle—the foundation of all you are, all you do, all you have, and of all you are becoming.

august 3

WHAT THE WORLD needs is a new generation of the people of God who are prepared to abandon the materialism of these modern times. Men and women who know the value of a soul in the context of now and eternity. Men and women who are able to raise their eyes from the things of this world to the greater things of the next world. People who allow Heaven and earth to meet each day in their prayer and in every activity of their lives.

Making resolutions is an important part of the journey of any struggling soul. Resolutions give our hopes, goals, dreams, and vision direction and practicality. There are some basic guidelines for making resolutions. Make only a few resolutions, preferably one at a time. Write each resolution down. Resolve first to perform your duties and obligations. Examine yourself with regard to your resolution early in the morning and before you retire at night. Do what you resolve. P.S. And when you fail, do not quit. Trust in God, humble yourself, and renew your resolution. Your family, your church, your society, your country, and your world need people who are prepared to accept the responsibility of change.

august 4

———

ARE YOU GOING to be a pilgrim or are you going to be a tourist? Tourists want everything to go exactly as they have planned and imagined it. They rush around from one place to another making sure they cram everything in . . .

Pilgrims are very different. They look for signs. If a flight gets delayed or canceled, they ask, "What is God trying to say to me?" Pilgrims are not concerned with seeing and doing everything, just the things they feel called to see and do. Pilgrims go looking for meaning. Pilgrims count their blessings. The reality is we are all pilgrims. This planet we call earth is not our home; we are just passing through. We build homes and establish ourselves here on earth in ways that ignore that we are really just here for a short time. That's why the happiness that God wants and created us for is very different from the fleeting happiness and momentary pleasures of this world.

august 5

THE PROBLEM is we value some people more than other people. Jesus doesn't do that. If a hundred people died in a natural disaster in our city, this would capture our attention for days, weeks, months, or even years. If a thousand people died on the other side of the world, we might barely think of it again after watching the story on the news.

Why do we value American lives more than African lives? Why are we comfortable with Asian children sewing our running shoes in horrific conditions for wages that are barely enough to buy food? What is so important? Cheap shoes. Cheap clothes. Cheap drill bits. Cheap stuff.

Our quest for more and more of everything is affecting real lives. Our quest for the cheapest of everything is literally killing people in other parts of the world. Those people over there, in other countries, whom we so easily place apart from us, are men and women just like you, with hopes and dreams. And they have children, just as precious to them as your children are to you. Our cheap stuff comes with a price tag: heartache and suffering. Jesus wants to challenge our attitudes and behaviors toward things, because they affect our attitudes and behaviors toward people.

august 6

THERE IS SOMETHING about travel that reminds us that we are just passing through this place we call Earth. It is easy to forget that essential truth, and when we do, our value and lives become distorted. We are pilgrims on a journey. Life is a pilgrimage, but sometimes we need to journey to gain perspective, so we can live our one life to the fullest.

The saints made regular retreats and pilgrimages. These experiences tend to powerfully align us with God and give us the courage to press on. Otherwise it is so easy to become paralyzed by fear.

What are your fears? Why are we so afraid to do what we love? What fear is holding you back the most at this time in your life?

august 7

IF WE REDUCED the world's population to one hundred people, proportionally, this is how the world would look: Fifty-seven of those one hundred people would come from Asia, twenty-one from Europe, nine from Africa, eight from North America, and five from South America . . . Six of those one hundred people would own or control more than 50 percent of the world's wealth, and five of these six people would be U.S. citizens.

A simple sketch like this challenges the way we see the world, and draws us out of our own little world. Our worldview constantly needs challenging. Your worldview is made up of a million thoughts, ideas, beliefs, and prejudices. It is unique to you, and largely formed by your past experiences and education. For these reasons your worldview has blind spots and is imperfect. My worldview is distorted and imperfect in the same way. These blind spots and distortions cause us all sorts of problems in life, especially in relationships. This is why God is constantly challenging our worldview.

august 8

THE KEY to repositioning Christianity as an incredibly positive and powerful force in our culture is what I like to call a 100 percent issue. A 100 percent issue is one that no reasonable, rational man or woman of goodwill can disagree with. For example, I believe no child in the United States should go to bed hungry. That's a 100 percent issue. If we came together as Christians, united as one force, regardless of our denominations or theological differences, we would lead the charge, and the social and political pressure for every other group in the country to join us in the effort would be overwhelming and undeniable. Even groups, like Fortune 500 companies and the United Way, that increasingly shy away from supporting faith-based initiatives would be under tremendous pressure to participate. We would end childhood hunger in America. In the process we could completely change the image of Christianity in this country and around the world. We would no longer be seen as a massively divided people who mostly talk about doing good things; we would be seen as modern leaders committed to changing the world one problem at a time.

august 9

_____

I REMEMBER the first time I heard the story about Jesus going into a village and healing all the people who were sick and hurting. The next morning, he woke before dawn and went alone to a quiet place to pray and regain his strength. Later Peter came running to him and said, "Everyone in the village is looking for you." Most people would go down into the village square, allowing themselves to be showered with gifts and praise, basking in their glory.

Most people would be shaking hands, kissing babies, and signing autographs. But not Jesus. He had a very clear sense of who he was and the mission before him. So he told Peter and the others, "Let us go to the other villages, so that I may speak there also. It is for this that I have come." Now, that is a statement of purpose and clarity.

august 10

_____

EMPTY YOURSELF so that God can fill you up. You will never be sorry that you did. I have experienced the emptiness of selfishness, and I have experienced the ecstasy of emptying myself so that God could fill me. The first is like drinking salt-water to quench your thirst; the second is like drinking deeply from the purest water you have ever tasted. For the first time in my life, I felt truly satisfied. I yearn for you to experience that same satisfaction. Strip away everything that makes you less available to God. This process of stripping everything else away is one of the defining experiences as we enter deeply into the inner life.

Prayer is ultimately about making ourselves available to God. So is life. Through prayer our spiritual awareness is constantly fine-tuned, and the more fine-tuned it becomes, the more we come to see that so few things really matter. The challenge, then, is to focus on the things that really matter. Is your life focused on the things that matter most? I am ashamed to say that too often I ask myself this question and the answer is no. Make space for God in your life.

august 11

RESPECT BUILDS trust. We nurture this respect in two ways. First, simply learning to enjoy people. Taking the time to get to know them, listening more and speaking less, seeking to understand rather than to be understood. By accepting other people for who they are with all their quirks, understanding that they have had a different experience of life and that those different experiences have contributed to make them who they are today. With every encounter, seek to know people more: who they are, where they come from, what their story is, what their passions are, what are their hopes and dreams.

The second way we nurture respect is by taking time each day to sit in the classroom of silence, to reflect on the true value of people and things. Some people spend time in the classroom of silence by taking a long walk in a quiet place, others spend time in the quiet of their church; some have a big comfortable chair in a corner of their home that serves as their classroom of silence. But one thing is common to all of us: silence makes us take a look at who we are, where we are going, and the value we assign to relationships and things.

august 12

THE CRY of every person's heart is a cry for happiness. More than ever people are searching in all the wrong places for the happiness they so desire. The most common mistake is to search for happiness in pleasure and material gain. This search is in vain; any happiness that comes from the pleasure of the flesh disappears as soon as the activity producing the pleasure ceases. Any happiness that comes as a result of material possessions vanishes if the material possession is removed.

The happiness that we should be concerned with as children of God is not the happiness of a healthy animal or the happiness of a person who has all he wants but a fulfillment deep within our hearts that pours forth peace, joy, and serenity. This happiness is not affected by the feelings and emotions that fluctuate through our bodies from one moment to the next. This happiness is not affected by the changing external circumstances of our lives. This happiness is a constant, the result of uniting our consciousness with the Spirit and every moment of our everyday lives with God. This is the only true happiness, and it is achieved through prayer.

august 13

———

AS WE GROW in maturity, we become aware of two important realizations. The first is that people are not born with beliefs and opinions; these are the result of education and experience. Therefore people's beliefs and opinions are constantly being refined as they are exposed to new experiences and ongoing education.

The second is that belief is something that evolves in our lives. Have you always believed exactly what you believe today? Of course you haven't. You have developed your beliefs in response to the education and experiences that you have been exposed to along the way. And there is a very good chance that your beliefs will continue to change as you grow in intellectual and spiritual maturity in the years to come. We all have the capacity to believe, and what we believe affects the way we live our lives. We are not born with beliefs. They are developed along the way. Taken on and discarded. Lived and tested. Abandoned and betrayed. Belief is at the essence of being human, so we cannot earnestly seek to become perfectly ourselves and ignore the role belief plays in our lives.

august 14

_____

A LOT OF THE dissatisfaction we experience in this lifetime comes from forgetting that we are made for mission. God didn't create us to be served; he created us to serve. If you use something for a purpose it was not designed for, things usually start to go wrong. Have you ever tried to use a snow blower as a vacuum cleaner? Right, that's a stupid idea. Have you ever tried to use a fire extinguisher to take a shower? Right, another stupid idea. Using things for something other than what they were specifically designed for usually ends up pretty ugly. But we do it with ourselves all the time. God designed human beings for specific purposes. When we stray from them, things tend to go wrong and we start to feel dissatisfied at best and miserable at worst. You were made for mission. You will never have lasting happiness until you realize this and act on it.

august 15

———————

THERE ARE FOUR words that embody the challenge of the Christian life; we find them in the fifth line of the Our Father: Thy will be done. These four words present the greatest challenge of Christianity. How do you react to these four words? What do they make you think? How do they make you feel? When you first read them, how did your body react?

It all depends on our image of God. If we see God as "far away," trying to control everything and everyone, we probably react to these words as an infringement on our personal freedom. If we see God as a loving father who wants good things for us even more than we want them for ourselves, who always has our best interests at heart, then we react very differently. For this reason, it is important that we constantly reflect upon our image of God. How we see God has an enormous impact on our lives. Our image of God is the lens through which we see ourselves, others, and the world. Our spirituality is particularly impacted by the way we see God.

august 16

IT IS HERE that we stumble upon the source of our virtue: God and our relationship with him. It is said that God will never be outdone in generosity. Jesus speaks of a return of a hundredfold in this world and eternal life in the next (Mark 10:31). How generous are you with God?

I suppose it is hard to be generous with someone who has everything and needs nothing. And yet, like any loving parent, God yearns to be with his children. God yearns to be with us. He delights in spending time with us (Proverbs 8:31). One way we can be generous with God is by spending time with him. Not just the leftovers, the scraps of our day, but dedicating a specific time each day for prayer is one way to be generous with God . . .

But the hardest way for us to be generous with God is by surrendering to his will for our lives. "Thy will be done, on earth." That means in our daily lives. "Thy will be done." In everything we think, do, and say. Surrendering ourselves to the will of God is the Mount Everest of spirituality and a great opportunity for each of us to be generous with God.

Every day presents an endless string of opportunities to share the love of God with other people by being generous.

august 17

YOU CAN only choose to love. You cannot determine whether someone else will love you. But if in every situation you choose to love, nothing and no one can ever diminish you. Others may choose not to love you in return, but that doesn't diminish you. Their failure to love is their failure alone and diminishes only themselves.

When you choose not to love, you commit a grave crime against yourself. You may hold back your love to spite another person, or in an attempt to hurt another person. Withholding love is a bit like drinking poison and expecting the other person to die. You may hold back your love in the name of security or safety, but these are only illusions, and in time you will stand as a dwarf compared to the person you could have potentially become if you had chosen love.

Love is a choice. When we choose love, our spirit expands. When we choose not to love, our spirit shrivels.

august 18

THE MOST practical wisdom I have ever received about prayer was from an old priest many years ago, when I was first starting to take my spiritual journey seriously. The initial excitement had worn off and I was experiencing the early signs of dryness and desolation in prayer. Our natural and very human reaction is to wonder what we are doing wrong when prayer doesn't "feel good." We often aren't doing anything wrong, and prayer should never be judged by how it makes us feel. Prayer isn't about feelings.

"Just keep showing up," the old priest said to me. When I asked him what he meant, he replied, "I'm speaking plainly.

No hidden meanings, boy. Just keep showing up. Show up each day regardless of how you feel or if it is convenient.

Just show up and let God work on you."

The only failure in prayer is to stop praying.

august 19

I ENCOURAGED her to travel as early in her adult life as possible, explaining that "travel opens our minds to different cultures, philosophies, and worldviews. Travel opens our hearts to the people of foreign lands and their different traditions and creeds. Travel dissolves the stains of prejudice that infect our hearts and societies. Money spent on travel is money well spent on an education that you will never receive from a book or in a classroom."

august 20

STRENGTH OF character comes from prayer.Prayer enables us to get in touch with the deepest desires of our hearts. It allows us to go beyond our shallow and superficial desires and to discover what it is that we truly want.

As we begin to assess how we use our time and expend our energy, we will soon recognize the first and most basic truth, the underlying principle of the spiritual life: whatever you do to another you do to yourself.

Life is a turbulent river. I am standing in the middle with water up to my chest, facing upstream. Each day I throw my thoughts, words, and actions upstream. Eventually, whatever I put out comes straight back down the river of life and hits me in the face. Ultimately, in this life, and certainly in the final analysis, you get what you give. We break and separate. God heals and unites. We place God far away. God says to us, "I live in you and you live in me." We build fences between each other. God says to us, "You are all parts of the one body."

august 21

YOUR LIFE TODAY is an answer to the questions you have asked up until now. The good news is that you can change the questions anytime you wish. Ask better questions and you get better answers.

IF GOD gives you the grace of encouragement and inspiration, fabulous. Accept it, embrace it, put it to good use, and don't squander it. But if you come away from prayer discouraged on some days, remember that Jesus died on the cross and that was an immense victory. Still, don't see that as an invitation to a life of misery that you design for yourself by creating crosses that God never intended you to carry. Life will bring you enough suffering and challenges without you looking for more. Again, just keep showing up and God will teach you all these things and so many others. For myself, though there have been times when prayer has seemed effortless, for the most part it doesn't come particularly easily. There are days when I have more enthusiasm for it than other days. And there are days when it is difficult. It requires me to force myself to do it. And of course, there are days when it's wonderful and blissful. It all just depends on what God is doing. No matter what, just keep showing up. I find it helps if we remember, it is not about what we are doing. It's about what God is doing in us, through us, and with us—when we show up.

august 23

WE MIGHT discover that they were not advice givers, warners, or moralists, but the few who were able to articulate in words and actions the human condition in which we participate . . . Not because of any solution they answered, but because of the courage to enter so deeply into human suffering and speak from there. Neither Kirkegaard nor Satre nor Camus nor Hammarskjold no Solzhenitsyn has offered solutions, but many who read their words find new strength to pursue their own personal search. Those who do not run away from our pains, but touch them with compassion bring healing and new strength . . . In our solution-oriented world, it is more important than ever to realize that wanting to alleviate pain without sharing it is like wanting to save a child from a burning house without the risk of being hurt.

august 24

WHEN I WAS a child everyone asked, "What do you want to do when you grow up?" When I was in high school everyone asked, "What do you want to do in college?" When I was in college everyone asked, "What do you want to do when you graduate?" So I spent a lot of time thinking about what I wanted to do and a lot of time doing what I wanted to do. I quickly realized that satisfaction was not to be found in doing whatever I wanted to do . . .

As the years have passed other questions have emerged. How is the best way to live? How can I best engage my talents and abilities to make a contribution? What helps me become the-best-version-of-myself? How can I lighten the burden of those less fortunate than myself? Where do I find genuine satisfaction? But in truth, these questions have been slow in surfacing, and it has taken several cycles of chasing what I wanted with reckless abandon, achieving what I wanted, and experiencing a certain emptiness for me to take these other questions more seriously and make them a more constant part of my inner dialogue and reflection.

august 25

THE HARDEST LESSONS to learn in life are the ones we think we have already learned. Most people think they are good listeners, most people think they are good drivers, and most people think they are pretty good Christians. But compared to what? In reality, most people are not as good as they think they are at these things. The false perception is the result of illusory superiority. This is cognitive bias, whereby individuals overestimate their own qualities and abilities relative to others. From time to time it is good for us all to learn to listen again. Listen to those you love. Listen to your body. Listen to your conscience and soul. Listen to God.

august 26

WHEN YOU THINK of the word "discipline," what comes to mind? For many it is an overdemanding teacher or a controlling parent. Try to set that notion of discipline aside, and think of the discipline an athlete freely chooses to bring the best out of himself or herself. Nobody can give you discipline, or make you disciplined. Discipline is a gift we give ourselves. Every aspect of the human person thrives on discipline, and relationships are no different. Discipline is the price life demands for happiness. Again, I am not speaking about pleasure, I am talking about lasting happiness in a changing world. You cannot be happy for any sustained period of time without discipline. Discipline is the road that leads to fullness of life.

august 27

IT IS IMPORTANT to remember that God does all the heavy lifting in the spiritual life. All he asks us to do is open ourselves to him and cooperate. These six significant moments are markers along the way in your sacred journey. There will be other significant lessons, shifts, moments in your journey. These are not the only six. But they are six that we all experience when we take the journey of the soul seriously.

First: Begin the Conversation

Second: Ask God What He Wants

Third: Give Yourself to Prayer

Fourth: Transform Everything into Prayer

Fifth: Make Yourself Available

Sixth: Just Keep Showing Up!

There are no rules that say you have to be a certain age before you can embrace these great spiritual lessons. There are no worldly conditions or requirements. There is nothing preventing you from beginning to practice each of these epic spiritual lessons today. All you need to do is respond to the desire that the Holy Spirit is stirring in your soul right now.

august 28

MOTHERS HAVE a unique perspective. A spiritual insight that fatherhood has bestowed on me is that nobody sees the life of a child the way the child's mother does. I love Walter, but my wife will always have a unique perspective on his life. The only way for me to gain that perspective is to speak with her about it. And when I talk to her about her relationship with our son, it enriches not only my relationship with her, but also my relationship with Walter. If I don't talk to her about her perspective, I miss out on something of our son's life. In the same way, Mary has a unique perspective of Jesus' life, and our relationship with her enriches our relationship with Jesus.

august 29

THE WORST PART is, we are rushing east in search of a sunset. We know this truth, but we don't know what to do about it. More and more demands are made upon us every day. We feel as though our lives have a momentum of their own. This momentum continues to carry us forward at an alarming pace . . . but to where? . . . to what end?

Is all this activity that clutters our lives helping us, or is it hurting us?

We have more money and more choices, but less time. Less time to do the things that nurture well-being and less time to spend with the people who invigorate us.

What we have gained is clear. But what have we lost? Are we aware of the real cost? Have we even begun to measure the real cost? You cannot measure the cost of everything in dollars and cents.

august 30

"GOD IS LOVE." When God speaks to me, He speaks about the person I am and the person I can be. He draws on images of the ideal and encourages me to allow those images to emerge from within me. He does not want me to be someone else. He does not want me to be something that I am not. God wants me to be the person I am truly. He calls this holiness, or sanctity. Being a saint is about allowing the real you to emerge from within.

The compelling fact that shines through all God has told me is that truth is attractive. When you are true to yourself, you grow in holiness. When the truth shines in a person, no darkness can put that light out. This is the holiness to which, through the messages, God is calling me—and not only me but you and indeed every man and every woman. God calls us all to holiness, and holiness is synonymous with happiness.

august 31

THE MODERN conception of life respects only action. To be spending your time in a worthwhile manner, you must be doing or achieving something. The crudest and most basic measure of this attitude is moneymaking. This mindset affects even the way we spend our recreation time. People are so caught up in this obsession with action and activity, they feel they must be doing something constantly. Prayer is an inner activity. When you pray you take on the appearance of doing nothing. And because the fruits, benefits, and rewards of prayer are internal, you appear to be achieving nothing. Nothing could be further from the truth.

Not every person with their eyes closed is asleep, and not every person with their eyes open can see.

september

september 1

———————————

WHETHER THEY WERE young or old, educated or uneducated, rich or poor, healthy or sick, the saints all had one thing in common: Prayer had a central place in their lives. They had amazing friendships with God because they were men and women of prayer.

If you do nothing else with your life, develop and amazing friendship with God. Become a man or woman of prayer. This friendship will change the way you see yourself and the world. It will rearrange your priorities, as love always does. It will give you clarity and a joy that nobody can take from you.

We learn to live deeply by praying deeply. Find that place within you where you can connect with God, and start to spend time in that place every day. Find that place within you where you can discover more and more about the-best-version-of-yourself. Make your prayer time a sacred item on your schedule. Make it nonnegotiable.

Strong daily routines are life-giving, and prayer is the first of them.

september 2

PHYSICALLY—WE don't exercise regularly because we're too busy. We don't eat the right types of food, because they take too long to prepare, and we're too busy.

Emotionally—most of us know that the happiest people on the planet are those who are focused in their personal relationships. Relationships thrive under one condition: carefree timelessness. Do we gift our relationships with carefree timelessness? Of course we don't. We shove them into ten minutes here and fifteen minutes there when we are most tired and least emotionally available. Why? We are too busy.

Intellectually—we don't even take those ten or fifteen minutes each day to read good books that challenge us to change, to grow, and to become the-best-version-of-ourselves. Why? We don't have time. We are too busy.

Spiritually—most people very rarely step into the classroom of silence to reconnect with themselves and their God. Why? We are afraid we might be challenged to change. And we are too busy.

It begs the question, doesn't it? What are we all too busy doing?

september 3

TUCKED AWAY in our subconscious, we see ourselves on a long trip that spans the continent. We are traveling by train. Out the windows we drink in the passing scenes . . . But uppermost in our minds is the final destination. Once we get there so many wonderful dreams will come true and the pieces of our lives will fit together like a completed jigsaw puzzle. How restlessly we pace the aisles, waiting for the station.

"When we reach the station, that will be it!" we cry. "When I am 18." . . . "When I put the last kid through college." "When I get a promotion." "When I reach the age of retirement, I shall live happily ever after!"

Sooner or later we must realize there is no station, no one place to arrive at once and for all. The true joy of life is the trip. The station is only an illusion. It constantly outdistances us . . .

So stop pacing the aisles and counting the miles. Instead, climb more mountains, eat more ice cream, go barefoot more often, swim more rivers, watch more sunsets, laugh more, and cry less. Life must be lived as we go along.

september 4

THE REALITY is that to a certain extent, we can see into the future, and we can do something about it if we see something we don't like in our future. Thoughts create actions. Actions create habits. Habits create character. And your character is your destiny—in the workplace and in relationships. In every sphere of life, your character provides significant insight into your future.

At the core of character we find our habits. Character is not what someone says but what he or she actually does. Habits are the building blocks of character. What are your habits? What are the things you do every day, every week, or every month? If you can tell me what your habits are, I can tell you what your future looks like. The future is not something that happens to us. It is an external expression of our internal reality.

september 5

_____

TO LOVE DEEPLY, you must let go of those illusions of perfection, that pretense of being completely in control, and open yourself to that mysterious gift, pleasure, power, and grace we call love. That surrender and openness creates a radical vulnerability. Love is to step beyond the comfort zone.

My mother has always enjoyed her garden, but she particularly loves growing orchids. Mum has grown them in our backyard ever since I was a child. When my brothers and I were younger, we used to play a lot of soccer and cricket in the backyard. One of us was al- ways crawling toward the kitchen to confess the accidental assassination of one of Mum's orchids.

I overheard a conversation one night between my mother and father. My mother was venting that we were killing all her orchids. My father listened, and a little time passed before he said calmly, "Well, one day they won't be here to play in the yard and break the orchids. When that day comes we will wish they were, so let's move the plants."

september 6

THE FOLLOWING is a historical description of Jesus by Publius Lentulus, governor of Judea, addressed to Tiberius Caesar, emperor of Rome.

"There lives, at this time, in Judea, a man of singular virtue whose name is Jesus Christ, whom the barbarians esteem as a prophet, but his followers love and adore him as the offspring of the immortal God. He calls back the dead from the graves, and heals all sorts of diseases with a word or a touch. He is a tall man, and well shaped, of an amiable and reverend aspect; his hair of a color that can hardly be matched, the color of chestnut full ripe, falling in waves about his shoulders. His eyes bright blue, clear and serene, look innocent, dignified, manly and mature. In proportion of his body, most perfect and captivating. He rebukes with majesty, counsels with mildness, his whole address, whether in word or in deed, being eloquent and grave. No man has seen him laugh, yet his manner is exceedingly pleasant; but he has wept in the presence of men. He is temperate, modest and wise; a man, for his extraordinary beauty and divine perfections, surpassing the children of men in every sense."

september 7

THIS LEADS US straight to what may be the single largest deficiency in the work-life balance quest of the past twenty years: personal responsibility. Work-life balance, work-life effectiveness, personal and professional satisfaction—or whatever you choose to call it—is not an entitlement or benefit. Your company cannot give it to you. You have to create it for yourself. You are personally responsible for living the best life you can.

You are personally responsible for the speed of your life and your lifestyle. This is a frightening truth because it causes us to realize that we have chosen and created the life we are living right now. But while it may be frightening for us to think that we have chosen to live our life exactly as it is today, it is also liberating. Liberating because, while we may not like what we find when we look at our lives today, we can now begin to choose differently.

september 8

THE CENTRAL QUESTION in any discussion about divine Providence is: Do you trust that God will provide for you? Intellectually and theologically it is easy to say yes, but practically we prefer not to have to rely on God. Part of the reason is trust, but the other part is greed.

God's promise is that he will provide for our needs, not that he will provide for our greed. This is where our world collides with our neighbors'. When we place our wants before our neighbors' needs we abandon our post as stewards. There is plenty of food in the world to feed everyone, and yet more than two billion men, women, and children are hungry right now. And it is not just in foreign lands that people are hungry. More than 20 percent of children in the United States live in poverty. It is sobering to think that if we were willing to go without some of the things that complicate our lives or so many of the things that we don't really need, we would be able to save lives.

september 9

WHETHER YOU ARE sixteen or 116 years old, it doesn't matter. Make yourself 100 percent available to God and he will find a way to work powerfully through you. Your age is his problem. Now is your time.

So get out there and start creating some Holy Moments—one at a time, as many as you can each day—and together, let's bring a new hope to the people of our time. What would society look like if more and more people were focused on creating Holy Moments? The people of our time are hungry for hope; we cannot survive without this beautiful gift. Every Holy Moment gives someone, somewhere the gift of hope.

This world should be different because you were here.

september 10

IF YOU WANT to change the trajectory of your career, change the period of time you deal with and think about. If you want to change your life, change the period of time you think about.

So the first step is, don't be in too much of a hurry to create the ideal life you have imagined. Personal and professional satisfaction are built like a castle, one brick at a time. We tend to overestimate what we can do in a day and underestimate what we can do in a week. In the same way, we tend to overestimate what we can do in a year and underestimate what we can do in a decade.

Take the decade view. Give yourself a decade to build the life you have imagined for yourself, one that is rich and overflowing with personal and professional satisfaction. Until you take the decade view, until you begin to imagine and plan what you can do in a decade, you have not even begun to explore your potential.

september 11

ALONG THE WAY, be mindful that the spiritual life is not a straight line. It is not a checklist of items to work through.

Everyone does not encounter them in the same order. There will be steps forward and steps back. Learn from the steps back. It is also easy to regress from talking to God in prayer to just thinking about stuff. It is part of the journey. It is easy to slip back from asking God what he wants to telling him what you want. It is part of the journey. It is easy to revert from giving ourselves to prayer to mechanically doing our prayer. And there will be days when you take back all you have surrendered to God. It is all part of the journey.

In the spiritual life, ground that is won today can be easily lost tomorrow. For this reason, it is essential that we guard our hearts and remain ever vigilant of the people and things that seek to steal us away from what matters most. How? Place the daily habit of prayer at the center of your life. Make it a non-negotiable sacred daily commitment.

september 12

_____

BUT IN A deeply subconscious way, the explanation for why we don't read the Bible more is deeply profound: We know the Word of God has the power to transform our lives, and the uncomfortable, unspoken, and often-avoided truth is that we don't want our lives transformed. Be honest. Do you want God to completely overhaul your life and totally transform you?

Transformation may seem attractive in a moment of blissfully holy idealistic exuberance or at a moment of crisis, but the every day reality is we like to distance ourselves from the inner work required to bring about such a transformation.

The long history of God's relationship with humanity has always displayed his preference for collaboration over intervention. God will not snap his fingers and bring about the type of transformation we are talking about here. He desires a dynamic collaboration with each of us. God wants us to do our part.

So, no, we don't necessarily want our lives transformed. Sure, we want some tweaking, but not transformation. This desire for tweaking is selective and selfish, while transformation is total and selfless.

september 13

HAVE YOU EVER wondered what God looks for on a résumé? Only one thing! He asks only one thing of us. He can take care of the rest. It's like what Jesus did with the five loaves and the two fish. God wants to do that with your life. The one thing God needs from you in order to launch you into mission is availability. It's the only thing he needs from any of us. Make yourself available to God and incredible things will happen. How available are you to God at this time in your life? Twenty percent, 50 percent, 75 percent, 96.4 percent?

Talk about resistance. We are resistant to making ourselves 100 percent available to God. It's crazy when you think about it. We hold back from God because we want to be in control. This is one of the grandest delusions in human history. We are not in control, and we never will be.

september 14

WE SHOULDN'T stop celebrating progress. I am happier when I am making progress. Look back at times in your life when you have made progress in an area of your life. How did you feel about yourself, about life, and about your future?

Our capacity for improvement is unfathomable. But to improve, we need to know ourselves very well. We need to be able to look beyond our obvious strengths and weaknesses and see our subtle tendencies. We need to be able to detect when we are lying to ourselves, when we could give more than we are giving, and when we are truly heading down the wrong path.

Over the years as I have studied many different forms and expressions of spirituality. One of the few things I have become absolutely convinced of is that some type of daily examination is one of the fastest ways to growth. Those who have taken spiritual development most seriously for thousands of years have employed this simple exercise not to measure perfection but to gauge progress.

september 15

IN EVERY MOMENT of the day we must train ourselves to put character ahead of our own designs and desires. Putting character first means that we will allow our thoughts, decisions, actions, and relationships to become subordinate to this quest to become and remain authentic.

Character is the greatest investment any of us can make. Investing requires discipline, self-control, and patience. Many of us lack one or all of these qualities—and often we lack the wisdom and humility to ask God for his help. Think of it in the financial sense. If you saved one dollar a day from the age of twenty-two until the age of sixty-five and invested that money at an average return of 7 percent, you would retire with close to four hundred thousand dollars. Three dollars a day would give you a million dollars, and yet, most people retire with little or no net worth. Is it because they couldn't afford to set aside one, two, or three dollars a day, or is it because they lacked the discipline, self-control, and patience?Make character your number-one priority in every sphere of your life. Put character first.

september 16

FOR OVER five decades, Mother Teresa emerged as an icon of modern holiness, capturing the imaginations and intriguing the hearts and minds of people from every nation on earth. Dedicated to a life of simplicity, she gave herself to society's most marginalized victims. Her love for people was tangible. You could see it. You could feel it. You could reach out and touch it. It was real and living. It wasn't a sermon or a speech. Each moment, she looked only for the next opportunity to love. For her, every individual mattered. "I believe," she once said, "in person-to-person contact. Every person is Christ for me, and since there is only one Jesus, the person I am meeting is the one person in the world at that moment." Those who spent time with her would often comment, "For the moment you were with her, there was only you and her. She wasn't looking over your shoulder to see what was happening around you. You had her full attention. It was as if nothing else existed to her except you."

september 17

ONE OF THE GREAT challenges of the art of living
is to learn to discipline ourselves, but at this moment in history, gratification seems to be the master of most people's
hearts, minds, bodies, and souls. We find ourselves enslaved
and imprisoned by a thousand different whims, cravings,
addictions, and attachments. We have subscribed to the ad-
olescent notion that freedom is the ability to do whatever
you want, wherever you want, whenever you want, without
interference from any authority. Could the insanity of our
modern philosophy be any more apparent? Freedom is not
the ability to do whatever you want. Freedom is the strength
of character to do what is good, true, noble, and right. Freedom is the ability to choose and celebrate the-best-version-
of-yourself in every moment. Freedom without discipline
is impossible.

september 18

———————————

PATIENCE IS the ability to endure prevailing circumstances. Our practice of patience needs to extend to ourselves, our God, other people, and external situations. We should develop the ability to be patient with ourselves by not placing unreasonable expectations on ourselves and by being realistic about our abilities. Our patience should also be exercised in our relationship with God as we wait for Him to unfold His plan for us.

Perhaps the most difficult practice of patience involves other people. We all have our own way of doing things. Some people do things that just irritate us. Their actions seem irrational, or worse. In these situations our virtue is challenged. When we find ourselves irritated by other people and their ways, one way to soothe our irritation and transform it into understanding is to remember that we too at times irritate others by the way we do things.

september 19

FOR THE NEXT twenty-four hours, try not to judge a single person or situation. Give people the benefit of the doubt. Try to see the situation from where they sit. Practice non-judgment. Nonjudgment fosters open and honest communication and breeds intimacy. Judgment is death to intimacy.

Judgment is one of the great poisons that kill relationships. Begin each day with this affirmation: "Today I shall judge nothing that occurs." When you do find yourself judging people, places, things, circumstances, gently repeat the simple mantra, "Today I shall judge nothing that occurs."

You may very quickly find that both your inner and outer dialogue are littered with judgments. When I first tried this exercise, I was astounded and humbled by how many judgments enter into my heart and mind in the course of a single day. If this is what you discover, it may be helpful to break the day down into hours, repeating the mantra each and every hour: "For the next hour I will not judge anything that occurs."

september 20

THE MOST IMPORTANT things are hardly ever urgent. In each of the four areas of life (physical, emotional, intellectual, and spiritual) we know what is most important, but we tell ourselves that we will attend to those matters later, when we have finished with the urgent things. "I'll do it when I get caught up!" we tell others and ourselves. This might not be so much of a problem if we did actually do the most important things when we got caught up. But we don't. Not because we don't want to, but because we never get caught up. Seriously, when was the last time you sat down and you said to yourself, "I'm caught up now!"

It doesn't happen. Your to-do list just gets longer and longer every day. You never get caught up; you just get more and more behind every day. Because the most important things are hardly ever urgent, that is why we have to place them at the center of our lives. We have to put them on our schedules, because if we don't we simply won't get around to them. "Things which matter most must never be at the mercy of things which matter least" was Goethe's advice.

september 21

HUMOR IS essential to the human experience. Many of the most memorable and meaningful moments in life are humorous. But where is humor in our experience of God, religion, and spirituality?

If you read the life and teachings of Jesus as portrayed in the four Gospels, there is little evidence to suggest that he had a sense of humor. Do you believe that Jesus didn't have a sense of humor? I believe he had a wonderful sense of humor. I imagine him walking down the dusty roads of Galilee with his disciples. Thirteen guys spending all that time together. There must have been some epic moments of humor. Wouldn't you love to hear Jesus laugh? Wouldn't you love to know what made him laugh and how he made others laugh?

For some reason, nobody thought it was important enough to record, and we have been making the same mistake by excluding humor and laughter from our relationship with God ever since. Just as humor is essential to the human experience, maybe it is also essential to our spiritual experience.

september 22

WHEN I REFLECT on the life of Mother Teresa the questions I ask myself are: Where does this power to love so deeply come from? Where does the strength to serve so selflessly come from? What is the source of this woman's extraordinary ability to inspire? The answers to these questions are also deeply embedded in her life. Before everything else, Mother Teresa was a woman of prayer. Each day, she would spend three hours in prayer before the Blessed Sacrament. Her power to love, her strength to endure, and her gift to inspire the masses were all born in the classroom of silence. This woman believed in the centrality of Jesus Christ. She knew his centrality in history and eternity, and she trusted his centrality in her own life. There lies the source: She placed Jesus at the center of her life. In the depths of her heart, she knew that action without prayer was worth nothing.

september 23

_____

WE ARE ALL CALLED to holiness. We are all called to become the-best-version-of-ourselves. We can make all sorts of excuses about why we cannot, but that doesn't change the fact that the central goal of the Christian life is to love God and neighbor by living a holy life. When we lose sight of that, we become spiritually lost. Better to be physically blind than spiritually lost. God wants you to live an excellent life. In that quest for excellence you will find a rare happiness.

september 24

TODAY, IT IS common knowledge and practice that a rested field yields a plentiful crop. I wonder, the first time a farmer decided to let a field rest for a year, did his neighbors and friends say, "Oh, that's a clever idea"? Absolutely not. They laughed at him, made fun of him, talked about him behind his back, and thought he was crazy. The next year, when he brought in his crop from that field, he had the last laugh. The following year, when there were three or four fields resting, he smiled to himself with a gentle sense of quiet satisfaction. Ten years later, when every farmer in the district was using the resting field method, he had become a legend.

The cycles of nature hold the untapped power of our lives, too. As you begin to discover those cycles and live by them, your friends will think you are crazy for leaving the party early, or for passing up "an irresistible opportunity" at work, or for changing the way you spend your Sunday. But over the weeks, months, and years ahead, as you bring the harvest of your life to be weighed, they will soon see that your way is better. They will turn to it. They too will begin to seek the rhythm of life.

september 25

HUMILITY CONSISTS of recognizing two simple truths at the same time: first, our nothingness, imperfection, and sinfulness; and second, God's greatness and the great things He can do in and through us. We are instruments. A paintbrush doesn't take the praise for a masterpiece; the artist does.

Think of it like this: you and I are simply vessels. If by some chance the Divine Gardener has laid His hands on us and placed us in His garden, filled us with the richest of soils, and in those soils has planted many beautiful seeds, and if from one of the seeds has grown a beautiful tree from which come wonderful fruits while from the other seeds many pretty flowers put forth wonderful fragrances and splendid colors—what have you and I had to do with the fruit, the fragrance, or the color? Nothing. We are just the vessel. We are instruments in the hands of God. The question is, are we prepared to let God use us?

Surrendering your life to God is about making yourself available for Him. God works many wonders in the lives of those who make themselves available to Him.

september 26

SAINT THERESE OF LISIEUX believed that love is expressed through attention to the small things that fill our daily lives. Mother Teresa practiced "the little way" taught by Therese.

This connection demonstrates that every act of holiness is a historic event. Every time we choose to love God and neighbor we change the course of human history, because our holiness echoes in the lives of people in other places and other times. Therese entered the convent at the age of fifteen and died at age twenty-four, but her influence continues to resonate in the lives of more than forty-five hundred Missionaries of Charity (the order Mother Teresa founded) who work in 133 countries today. It is impossible to measure Saint Therese of Lisieux's impact on history, but it is vast. Holiness is deeply personal, but it is also communal and historic. Holiness is not something we do for ourselves; it is something God does in us if we cooperate. And it is something he does in us not for us alone, but for others and for all of history.

september 27

———————

WHY IS THE human spirit so energized by sports? The reason is that sports are a microcosm of the human experience; they are an opportunity to have other human beings challenge us to change, to grow, to improve ourselves, and to explore our potential. We love to participate in sports and we love watching others participate, because in sports we see the human drama unfolding before us. And that drama is the quest to better ourselves, to stretch beyond our limitations, to become the-best-version-of-ourselves—to achieve our essential purpose. When I look at stadiums filled with thousands of people watching baseball, football, and basketball, I see whole generations yearning for something they have lost—their essential purpose. Devotees may argue that one sport is inherently superior to another. I prefer to think of all sports as a chance for us to have other human beings push us to excel, and in this they are all equal.

september 28

———————

WE ARE CAPABLE of so much more than we think. You have no idea what you are capable of. None of us do. God is constantly trying to open our eyes to the amazing possibilities that he has enfolded in our being. The saints continue this work, encouraging us to explore all our God-given potential, not with speeches but with the example of their lives. When we have the courage to collaborate with God and pursue our truest self, he lights a fire within us that is so bright and warm, it keeps shining long after our days on this earth have come to an end. The lives of the saints have captivated the people of every age for this very reason.

september 29

_____

HOW AVAILABLE are you to God at this time in your life? Think on it. Pause. It is impossible to measure, but you have a sense. Are you 20 percent, 50 percent, 80 percent, 96.4 percent? What is holding you back from making yourself 100 percent available to God? What would it take for you to make yourself 100 percent available? What are you afraid of losing or missing out on? What are you unwilling to give up for God? What's the danger of making yourself 100 percent available to him? What is the downside of giving it a try and seeing what happens?

september 30

HOW WE SEE other people and the world is at the core of the human experience. The Gospel equips us with a new lens. Through this lens we see other people, God, the world, and ourselves in a fundamentally different way than we did before. This is the Jesus effect. It changes our priorities, and by elevating them, it transforms the way we live and who we become.

Are you thriving or just surviving? If you're not thriving, why not? Perhaps it is time to abandon man's ways and embrace God's. Sometimes people ask, "How will I know when I am embracing God's ways more?" It's a great question

october

october 1

WE ARE AT our best when we are grateful . . . One of the leading indicators of my own spiritual health is whether or not I am in a place of gratitude. I have observed this time and time again. When I get in a bad mood or become overwhelmed by a situation, I have usually lost the perspective of gratitude. Next time you are in a bad mood ask yourself if you are grateful. It is impossible to be grateful and be in a bad mood. It is when we step away from gratitude that we become irritable, restless, and discontented.

The world draws us into a conversation about all that we don't have, but God invites us into a conversation about all that we do have. Which of those conversations is bouncing around your head today?

october 2

———————

I LIKE COMFORT—and there is so much comfort available. It is so easy to make comfort a priority in our lives. This leads to comfort addiction. Then even the slightest discomfort makes us irritable, restless, and discontent. Before long we are becoming one of those people who burst into an angry rage over the tiniest thing.

A couple of weeks ago, I was speaking with a friend, and he said something that really made me stop and reflect: "Everybody is looking for an easier, softer way." It's a generalization. It may not be true for everyone. But it sure seems true for most people. We want life to be easier. We want the path we walk to be softer. We want to be comfortable . . .

Why doesn't Jesus want us to get comfortable? The reason is simple, profound, and practical: He doesn't want us to forget that we are just passing through this world. We are pilgrims. When we get comfortable we start to behave as if we are going to live on this earth forever—and we are not.

october 3

SOME OF US are drawn into relationship with God early in life, others at the end of life, and some along the way . . . Were you drawn in into relationship with God early or later in your life? Are you feeling called to a deeper connection with him right now? Perhaps this is a special moment of grace for you.

So wherever you are today, I invite you to open yourself to God a little more by asking him to show you the power of his love. "Ask, and it will be given you; seek, and you will find; knock, and the door will be opened for you. For whoever asks receives, and everyone who searches finds, and for everyone who knocks, the door will be opened" (Matthew 7:7-8).

october 4

THERE ARE FOUR simple steps that will empower you to make a difference in other people's lives and lead you along the path of greatness.

STEP ONE: When you wake up tomorrow morning, remind yourself of your goal, your point B, your essential purpose—to become the-best-version-of-yourself.

STEP TWO: The next step is to ask yourself, "Whose day can I make today?"

STEP THREE : Now ask yourself, "How can I make that person's day?"

STEP FOUR : When you have made these first three steps, shower and have breakfast, but then, just before racing into the day, take a few minutes to plan, reflect, and pray. Find a quiet place, and in that silence visualize how you would like your day to unfold. Make plans to fulfill your legitimate needs physically, emotionally, intellectually, and spiritually. Take a moment to become aware of, and to appreciate, all you have and all you are, and then you will be ready for the day.

october 5

———————

SO WHY DID their colleagues single them out as champions of work-life balance? The answer is because, as it turns out, with almost all of them, they have large quantities of what this book is really about—personal and professional satisfaction. They work hard, but they have a sense of satisfaction when they leave the office after a long day. This professional satisfaction is fueled by several factors: they enjoy the people they work with; they feel respected by their boss; they feel their work is making a contribution to customers' lives; they find the challenge of their work matches their abilities; and they know why they go to work each day. This last one is critical, and it provides the segue into the personal realm.

You see, people don't come to work because they love their company, their work, or their boss. They may love all these things, but these are not the primary reasons they come to work. People come to work because they have dreams for themselves and for their families. And those who are achieving high levels of personal and professional satisfaction know what those dreams are.

october 6

TRUTH AND JOY are proportionally linked in our lives. The more we live truth, the more we experience joy. It cannot be put any other way. If you do what you know to be good and true, you will experience joy beyond compare. If you ignore the voice within you that is calling you to the ways of truth and love, you will be miserable and you will spread that misery. As we live the truth, so shall we love and be loved. Truth lived increases our ability to love and our ability to be loved. Holiness, I have learned, is about living the truth. Patience, kindness, humility, gentleness, and fortitude are all truths. And where there is truth, there is goodness, peace, joy, and love.

october 7

PART OF EVERY successful person's work process is an examination of best practices. Wherever you find excellence, you find a hunger for best practices. Too many people want to do things their way rather than the best way. It doesn't matter how you prefer to do something. What matters is outcome. What way of doing things will produce the most mission impact?

Every day we encounter dozens of opportunities, both personally and professionally, to engage the principle of best practices. Leveraging this principle creates a tremendous advantage, increases our chances of success, drives excellence, saves time, and improves results. Activating a curiosity about best practices should be the first task for every one of our projects. Who is the best in the world at this and what can I learn from her? Drive this behavior deep into your work process and deep into the work process of every member of your team and organization. It's time to stop talking about best practices and actually leverage this powerful principle in everything we do.

october 8

DO WE REALLY believe that a life without structure or discipline will yield the happiness we desire? Besides, how successful do you suppose your business would be if you just did whatever you wanted whenever you wanted to? What sort of financial shape would you be in if you bought whatever you wanted, whenever you wanted it? How good would your health be if you ate as much as you wanted, of whatever you wanted, whenever you wanted it? How healthy would your relationships be if you did what you felt like doing only when you felt like doing it?

A life without self-discipline doesn't lead to happiness—it leads to ruin. Every area of our life—physical, emotional, intellectual, spiritual, professional, and financial—benefits from self-discipline. Does that mean we should never engage in instant gratification? No. But it does mean that we cannot allow instant gratification to guide and direct every decision. We need to move beyond the notion that discipline is someone else telling us what to do and celebrate the self-discipline that liberates us. How much discipline is enough? The answer depends on how happy you want to be, and for how long you want that happiness to last.

october 9

THERE ARE AN unlimited number of people and situations to pray for by offering your work one hour at a time. In this way we bring unimaginable value to our work.

Some work has enormous intrinsic meaning, such as being a kindergarten teacher or working to cure cancer. But it is harder to see the meaning and value of selling widgets or serving burgers. When work is transformed into prayer, an hour of labor by someone who is serving burgers but offering it to God has more meaning and value than an hour by a brain surgeon who is only focused on how much money he will make for each surgery . . .

Christianity is incredibly practical. It is a beautifully human invitation to experience the divine. For a Christian, everything is a prayer. Eating is a prayer. Sleeping is a prayer. Exercising is a prayer. Waiting is a prayer. Traveling is a prayer. Making love is a prayer. Working is a prayer. Resting is a prayer.

God loves ordinary things. The culture fills our hearts and minds with spectacular dreams about hitting home runs, but life is about getting up every day and hitting a single.

october 10

WHAT PERCENTAGE of your church's activities take place on church property? In most cases the answer is more than 90 percent. In far too many cases the answer is 100 percent. We have built some amazing church facilities and campuses, and that is a good thing. But the mentality that accompanies these amazing facilities can be a country club mentality rather than one of a Christian community that is mission driven and passionate about transforming the world starting right there in your suburb, city, or state. What is your church community doing to reach the un- churched? If the answer is little or nothing, you probably have something that resembles a country club more than a church.

If we are serious about transforming the culture, we need to get out in the culture. We need to stop spending so much energy trying to get people to come to us, and get out among the people. That's what Jesus did. It is time to get out and reengage the people of our time with a fascinating conversation about life, death, eternity—but first we need to talk to them about whatever they are struggling with right now.

october 11

_____

AS FOR BELONGING to a vibrant community, we each have a role in creating that reality. In the past I have raised two questions: (1) There are seventy million Catholics in America. If we multiplied your life by seventy million, what would the Church in America be like? (2) There are more than a billion Catholics around the world today. If they were all like you, what would the Church be like?

Now let's focus these questions locally for a moment. It seems to me that everyone wants to belong to a dynamic parish. Even the people who only come to church at Christmas want to come to a dynamic parish and have a dynamic experience. Is your parish dynamic? Many are not. But the question is, what are you and I going to do about it? How are you willing to participate and contribute to your parish to help it become more dynamic each year?

If every person in your parish were as engage or disengaged as you, how dynamic would your parish be?

october 12

MAINTAINING CHARACTER requires constant vigilance and discipline. It is almost impossible if we allow fatigue and stress to settle into our lives permanently. At the same time, maintaining character demands that we stop chasing the false self and let go of all ego-driven behavior.

It requires strength and surrender, which can seem paradoxical, but it is not. Deep in our souls we need to know when maintaining character requires strength. For example, when injustice demands that we stand up for those who cannot stand up for themselves. But we also need to know deep in our souls when maintaining character requires complete surrender. For example, when we realize we are following the false self down a wayward path to satisfy some disordered ego need.

What we believe affects everything: how we live, how we work, how we feel about ourselves, and how we feel about others.

october 13

I OFTEN WONDER where I would be today if someone had not taught me how to pray. It scares me. I look back on those days when I was a teenager, spending all those hours with God in church. It was an amazing time in my life. Today, I cannot spend that kind of time in prayer. More to the point, I am not called to spend that much time in prayer, and you may never be called to do so. It was a season in my life, a season with a reason. Maybe I will have another season like that later in my life. I don't know, though I do yearn for it.

Being willing to go to the deep places is not about the amount of time we spend set apart from daily activity in prayer. Going to the deep places with God is about trusting him, making ourselves available to him, committing to a habit of daily prayer, and being mindful of his presence in each moment throughout the day. He wants to laugh with you and cry with you, listen to you and speak to you.

Ask God to draw you deeper into the mysteries of the spiritual life. It is a request he will not refuse, and the wonders he will reveal to you will leave you awestruck—and change your life forever.

october 14

_____

WHAT DOES GOD'S laughter sound like? It sounds like the smile of a newborn baby; it sounds like a bird flying high in the sky; it sounds like the anticipation of a first kiss; it sounds like a new beginning, a fresh start, the morning breeze; it sounds like the love of the most amazing father you could ever imagine; it sounds like a long drink of cold water after a day in the scorching sun; it sounds like the beach and the mountains; it sounds like the roar of a lion, and the gentle touch of a mother as her child rests. When God laughs, all your senses become one and your whole being radiates joy from the depths of your soul.

It is impossible to describe, and like you and I, God has many laughs, one perfectly suited for each situation. But we can be sure that the God who created us to have a marvelous sense of humor also has a marvelous sense of humor and loves to laugh.

How does hearing God laugh change you? It brings startling clarity to your life about what matters and what doesn't. It fills you with a desire to love God more than anything on this earth, and to accomplish that by loving people more than they love themselves.

october 15

WE ALL HAVE routines, rituals, and rhythms that are negative. They have power over us. They have central places in our story. They stop us from becoming the-best-version of ourselves. These negative patterns are so easy to fall into. Everything bad is a distortion of something good. Routines, rituals, and rhythms are a powerful force for good in our lives. They are central to creation, and therefore part of God's ingenious plan for you and me. What are the positive patterns in your life? They may be simple and seemingly insignificant, but they glue your life together in a profoundly positive way. It could be driving your kids to school, reading the newspaper in your pajamas on Saturday, what you eat for breakfast, walking the dog, making love to your spouse, or reading before you go to bed. Each of these is an informal routine or ritual. They create powerful rhythms in our lives, and together these routines, rituals, and rhythms hold our lives together in ways we will probably never understand.

october 16

———————

A TREE WITH strong roots can weather any storm. If you have not done so already, the day to start growing those roots is today. Gratitude, respect, and discipline are three powerful ways to ground and nurture your relationships. But keep in mind also, that trees sway in the wind. They are not rigid. Even the largest and strongest trees sway when the wind blows. Allow for uncertainty; you can be sure it will come. Find the lesson in the unexpected; it has come to help you in your quest to become the-best-version-of-yourself. Try to enjoy mystery; it will keep you young.

The present culture despises uncertainty, and so we waste endless amounts of time and energy trying to create the illusion of security and attempting to control the uncontrollable. We curse the unexpected because it interferes with our plans, even though it often carries with it the challenge we need at that moment to change and to grow into a better-version-of-ourselves. In the same way, our culture has no time for mystery. If we cannot solve it or prove it, then we ignore it or discredit it.

"Life is not a problem to be solved, it is a mystery to be lived."

october 17

WE ALL HAVE an inner life. This consists of our thoughts and feelings, our hopes and dreams, our character and our relationship with God. We all have an outer life, which consists of the things we do, places we go, and things we build or own. We tend to focus on the outer life, but it is only a tiny fraction of our life. Much more takes place as part of the inner life. The outer life is an overflow of the inner life.

october 18

IN EVERY AGE, there are a small number of men and women who are prepared to turn their backs on popular culture and personal gain to embrace heroically the life Jesus outlines in the Gospels. These people fashion Catholicism into a lifestyle, they listen attentively to the voice of God in their lives, and they passionately pursue their personal adventure of salvation. As a result, they capture the attention and the imaginations of everyone who crosses their path. Paradoxically, the modern world tends to pity these people, because it believes they are missing out on something. Never feel sorry for them. These men and women are the happiest people who ever lived. They are the heroes of Christianity; they are the saints.

october 19

_____

IT IS IN the deep places that we are finally able to contemplate life, ourselves, and God, and all three are worthy of contemplation. To contemplate is to reflect upon something with depth and at length. Spending time in the deep places with God allows us to focus our hearts, minds, and souls on the things that matter most. What we think about, reflect upon, and contemplate, has an enormous impact on the events of our lives and the state of our souls. Paul counsels us, "Whatever is true, whatever is honorable, whatever is just, whatever is pure, whatever is pleasing, whatever is commendable, if there is any excellence and if there is anything worthy of praise, think about these things (Philippians 4:8)." Rushing here and there, throughout the course of our busy days, does not give us time to reflect on these higher things. The majority of messages the world shares with us lead us away from these higher things. For these and all the many other reasons we have discussed, God beckons us to spend a portion of our day with him contemplating the higher things.

Don't be afraid of the deep waters of the spiritual life. It is there that the most amazing experiences await you.

october 20

_____

THE WAY OF TRUTH is a lifestyle. It is not a part-time occupation or hobby. It is not just one aspect of your life—it is your life. It is a way of approaching each circumstance that this life puts before you. Those who have lived such a life of holiness have told us that the only way to understand the true value of things in this life is to place them against the backdrop of eternity. It is then that we are able to see things in their proper perspective.If this were the only life and you did not possess an immortal soul, I would encourage you to seek pleasure and avoid pain. This, however, is not the only life, and you do possess an immortal soul as well as your sensory body, so I encourage you to use your mind, your will, and your intellect to allow your soul to be the master of your body. Train your body to be directed by the soul. For the soul is eternal, and that which is eternal should lead that which is temporal.

This process has a cost, and yes, it is painful. You will have to pass up some of the pleasures of this world, but never forget, it is for your own good. Every thought, word, and action in this life has eternal consequences.

october 21

———————

SINGLENESS OF purpose . . . it was precisely with this in mind that Ignatius of Loyola established his First Principle and Foundation: Man is created to praise, reverence, and serve God our Lord, and by this means to save his soul. The other things on the face of the earth are created for man to help him in attaining the end for which he is created. Hence, man is to make use of them in as far as they help him in the attainment of his end, and he must rid himself of them in as far as they prove a hindrance to him.

Therefore, we must make ourselves indifferent to all created things, as far as we are allowed free choice and are not under any prohibition. Consequently, as far as we are concerned, we should not prefer health to sickness, riches to poverty, honor to dishonor, a long life to a short life. The same holds for all other things.

Our one desire and choice should be what is more conducive to the end for which we are created.

october 22

———————

IT IS WHEN we begin to lose a grip on our humanity that the long betrayal of self begins. This betrayal always ends with us turning our backs on God, hurting other people, and engaging in some form of self-destruction. It is by running toward God that we run toward our true selves. It is our faith that empowers us to walk with God by loving the people who cross our paths and celebrating our best selves. And yes, this is something I want for my son.

Do I want my son to grow up and embrace the Catholic faith? Yes. I suppose all parents who take the spiritual life seriously want to pass on their particular religious' tradition to their children. But I don't want him to stay out of compulsion or guilt, and I certainly don't want him to stay to please his mother or me. I would like my son to immerse himself in the Catholic faith because somewhere deep within it resonates with him, speaks to him, moves him.

october 23

_____

CATHOLICISM is not a football game, but Paul once compared the Christian life to athletics, and I would like to continue the analogy. Championship winning teams are not necessarily those with the most talented players or the most ingenious new plays, nor are they necessarily the teams with the most resources or superior knowledge of the game. The very best coaches will tell you that teams that win championships are those that focus on the basics and master them together. We need to get back to the basics.

october 24

WE NEED to consider what stories we are telling our children. I am not talking about the stories we read young children before they go to bed, though these certainly play a powerful role in their development. I am talking about the stories we tell our children in conversation and through our example.

The most powerful story you tell the world every day is the story of how you choose to live your life. This story, your story, affects the lives of everyone who crosses your path . . . and millions of people whom you will never meet or know. Our lives are not a private matter; they are a public act with global repercussions. The way you live your life will be affecting people for generations to come until the end of time. What story are you telling with your life? This story will have more impact on your children than any other single factor in their lives.

Stories are powerful, and great leaders continuously develop an inspiring repertoire to have on hand when the right moment arises.

october 25

DO WE KNOW how to make choices? Are we aware of our choices when we are making them? Are we conscious that when we say yes to one thing we automatically say no to everything else? Did we ever really learn to make choices?

We make choices every day, hundreds of them. The ability to make good choices is critical to the success of our lives and our businesses. And yet, evidence suggests that few people have ever really been trained to make choices. And when we look at some of the choices people are making in their personal lives, shouldn't we cringe at the fact that they are probably using the same decision-making process to make choices that affect the future and destiny of our business? It seems to me that most of us need to learn how to make choices again.

octaber 26

THE WORLD SAYS that the preeminent question in your life is: What do you want? But life is not about getting what you want. At the same time, however, it is good, healthy, and important to know what you want.

Do you know what you want?

Do you spend time thinking about what you really want? If you're like most people, you don't have much time to spend thinking about anything. When was the last time you just took some time to go for a long walk or sit in a rocking chair and think about a single question? The most important things in life are almost never urgent. As a result, most people don't take the time to really think about life and don't truly know what they want.

You may say you want more money, a better job, to get married, to have a baby, to lose weight, a fabulous vacation ... but what is behind or beneath all this wanting?

Motives can teach us so much about ourselves. By studying our motives we can grow exponentially in the spiritual life.

october 27

_____

TERESA OF AVILA wrote about themes such as comfort and worry, how these things affect us, and how to deal with them. On the subject of comfort she wrote, "Our body has this defect that, the more it is provided with care and comforts, the more needs and desires it finds."

More comfort is available to us than at any other time in history, and yet still we crave more. Teresa had this awareness five hundred years ago—three hundred years before indoor plumbing and electricity were invented.

We know Teresa suffered significant cruelty at the hands of other people . . . And even though she had this astounding relationship with God, it is clear that she struggled with worry.

When she died, an old handmade bookmark was found in her prayer book, which she used to take everywhere with her. On the bookmark, Teresa had written, "Let nothing disturb you. Let nothing make you afraid. All things are passing. God along never changes. Patience gains all things. If you have God you will want for nothing. God alone suffices."

Someone who doesn't struggle with worry wouldn't write something like that. Someone who hadn't wrestled with fear wouldn't keep those words so intimately close at all times.

october 28

THE HAPPIEST people on the planet are the men and women who have dynamic relationships. This has been the one consistent discovery in my travels to more than fifty countries in the past ten years. No matter what continent you are on or what culture you are exploring, it stands as a self-evident and universal truth. The happiest people give focus and priority to their relationships, and as a result have a richer experience of relationship and of life.

Family is important to them; friendship is important to them. I have moved among the extremely well educated and the woefully uneducated. Educated people aren't happier than uneducated people. I have sat at meals with men and woman of extraordinary financial wealth and with those living in the cruelest poverty. The rich are not necessarily happier than the poor. I have lived among people who had seemingly little to worry about, people who had much to hope for in the future, and people under the death sentence of terminal illness and other tyrannies. The same truth is evident among all people, at all times, and in all situations: the happiest people are those who cherish the mystery of relationship.

WHAT IS THE ONE thing that God delights in above all else? Simply being with you. The delight of God is to be with his sons and daughters.

In any great relationship there is a time to talk about the ordinary things that occupy our days, a time to speak about more serious matters—decisions to be made and issues that weigh heavy on our hearts—and a time simply to be together. This wordless togetherness happens at the height of intimacy. There is no longer any need for ego or persona, no need to explain ourselves, and no need to understand or be understood. All that is set aside as we immerse ourselves in a great pool of acceptance.

God delights in you. He delights in just being with you. When we invite him into our lives he dances for joy. It helps to have tools and techniques to get us started in our journey of prayer, but ultimately, we have no need of artificial methods and complex systems. We are his children. Just talk to him and be with him. He is your Father and he loves you.

october 30

I BECAME fascinated with Thomas More for the first time when I worked as a stagehand for my high school's production of A Man for All Seasons. I was intrigued by this man who so obviously had his own life in his hands and yet chose to die. As the years have passed, I have grown more in awe of him. No one could accuse him of any incapacity for life. He embraced life, fully seizing every opportunity to explore its abundant variety. He loved deeply and was deeply loved. He was successful and admired. Thomas More was no plaster-cast saint; he was a man who loved life and was full of life. And yet, he found something within himself without which life is valueless. So when cruel and selfish men tried to take that something from him, he chose to embrace death rather than surrender to it. I hope you and I can find that something within ourselves.

october 31

WHEN JESUS WALKED the face of this earth, He did not ask people to fall down before Him in awe, to place Him on a pedestal, or to make a king or political leader of Him. In fact, He discouraged all of these responses. In the gospels we read that every time people tried to place Him on a throne and appoint Him as a great leader or ruler, He quietly moved on to the next place, although His heart no doubt ached because another city had failed to understand the message He was trying to convey. Jesus didn't want people to feel useless before Him; He wanted them to realize their true potential in Him. Yes, His divinity demands adoration, but Jesus wanted the greatest form of adoration. Jesus wanted the greatest form of worship. Jesus wanted the people to worship Him by imitating Him. Times have changed, but God remains eternally the same. Today Jesus wants the same perfect adoration as He did when He walked the earth—imitation. The greatest form of worship is imitation.

november

november 1

_____

SOMETIMES THE BEST way to reflect upon the story of our lives is to ponder death. Life is wonderful but short. The saints meditated on death so that they wouldn't take a moment of this precious life for granted. Life has a tendency to slip through our hands like water, unless we live each day, each hour, each moment with great consciousness. The saints nurtured this conscious awareness with daily prayer . . .

All lives are measured in the end—it serves us well to remember that—and it is men and women like Thomas More who inspire us to live courageously even in the face of great opposition. This is perhaps when and where the saints are most helpful to us, when times are tough. They demonstrate how to behave in the face of adversity, injustice, and even cruelty. And of course, they learned how to courageously encounter adversity by patiently reflection on the way Jesus lived his life.

The saints teach us to live boldly by listening to that gently voice within. Are you living the one short life you have been given with passion and purpose?

november 2

————————

IN SOME WAYS, I suppose we are not really ready for life until we have learned to be comfortable alone in the great classroom of silence. For it is out of the silence that clarity emerges . . .

You know this instinctively. If you are taking a road trip with a car full of people and you get lost, what does the driver ask everyone to do? Turn off the radio and be quiet. Why? When you need laser clarity you want silence. Lots of people who work listening to music turn the music off when they really need to concentrate on something. Why? Clarity emerges from silence. And people who live with high levels of passion and purpose are not afraid of spending some time alone in silence to work out who they are, what they are here for, and what matters most.

In this way it seems that God is always saying to me, "Come to the quiet." The world is noisy and distracting. It is in the silence that we find God and our true self.

november 3

GOD WANTS US to be like Him. What are you capable of? Do you want to be great? What is the greatest thing you can do? The greatest act available to you is to be like God. In prayer we come to know the ways of God. When these ways become a part of a person's life, we call them virtues. God places these virtues in our hearts through meditation and reflection; once there, they will emerge throughout the day in our words, thoughts, and actions.

What is prayer? It is the process that leads men and women to become more like God.

If we are to become more like God, this, of course, presupposes changes. As we come to prayer, we must approach God with an openness to change. As long as we are not prepared to change, prayer will achieve nothing in our lives, and we will be ruled by selfish passions and live in anxious unhappiness. Any joy in our lives will be short lived.

Since prayer is about becoming more like God, the first step must be to get to know the God we are going to imitate. As our model we have been given Jesus, who is both true

november 4

———————

IN OUR QUEST for enduring happiness, it is important that we constantly remind ourselves that happiness is not achieved by the pursuit of happiness but rather is the result of right living. Right living, a life of integrity, is achieved by living through our daily actions all the good things we believe. You cannot leave your ethics and beliefs at the door of your workplace and still hope to live a life of harmony and unity. You cannot set certain values and beliefs aside when you are socializing with certain friends and hope to maintain your inner peace. Character and beliefs are part of the very fabric of our being. And when we treat them as optional accessories or disposable, we create deep divisions within ourselves.

Personal integrity—living by our beliefs, proactively willing the good of others, doing what we say we will do—is at the very core of unity of life. How then does one begin to create this unity of life?

We begin by turning to God in prayer.

november 5

WHEN YOU ARE discouraged or caught up in procrastination, simply do the tiniest thing to move whatever you are working on forward. Few can imagine just how powerful perseverance is. There is another quote that I like to reflect on from time to time, written by Calvin Coolidge, the thirtieth president of the United States: "Nothing in the world can take the place of persistence. Talent will not; nothing is more common than unsuccessful men with talent. Genius will not; unrewarded genius is almost a proverb. Education alone will not; the world is full of educated derelicts. Persistence and determination alone are omnipotent."

november 6

FROM TIME TO TIME, it is good for us to ask ourselves, "Is my life working?" It's a question I have asked myself many times throughout my life, and more than once the answer has been no. But I have never been sorry that I stumbled upon the question and found the courage to explore it.

Every time I have been nudged and realized my life wasn't working, being too busy has been part of the problem. Busy is not our friend. It makes us feel overwhelmed, tired, and inadequate. If busy were a person, would you spend all day with that person today, and then all day with that person again tomorrow? Busy is not your friend. This is a lesson I have had to learn too many times in my life. I fall into the common trap of overscheduling and overcommitting myself, and it usually happens when I am neglecting my daily habit of prayer.

november 7

———————

PERSONAL PRAYER is a deepening of your relationship with God, discovering who God is calling you to be for him and for others. The liturgical prayer of Sunday Mass is the prayer of the whole Church gathered as a public proclamation of who we are as Catholics. What you bring to Mass on Sunday is your prayer life, and the deeper it is, the more deeply you can enter into the public expression of the faith of the Church. The Mass is not simply about you; it is the whole Church gathered as a sign of hope to the world. A community at prayer is a beautiful thing.

november 8

PRAYER IS about uncovering and discovering truths—small truths and large truths, truths about ourselves and truths about our God. Life is about allowing the truths we discover about our God to emerge within us and become truths about ourselves.

The primary way in which we come to know God and His ways as Christians is through the Scriptures. Specifically the gospels are the revelation of Christ's life to all people. They tell us what He did and what He said, and they inspire us to act and speak in the same ways. Ignorance of the gospels is ignorance of Christ, as you cannot imitate someone you do not know.

Through the gospels we are fed. In thousands of ways we catch glimpses of God, and these at the same time reveal our faults and flaws. The gospels are thus always new and exciting. They probe the hearts of every man and woman and call us to the struggle to better ourselves.

november 9

IN ORDER TO consistently experience the happiness and joy God wants to fill us with we need to build a throne for truth in our lives. There is a direct relationship between truth and happiness. Truth leads to happiness. Lies bring misery. Celebrate truth in your life. What place does it have in your life? Are you willing to speak truth even at great personal cost? Are you able to acknowledge truth, even if you cannot live up to it? Even if we cannot do something that is good, even if we willfully and sinfully choose to do something that is wrong, we should still try to acknowledge what is good and true, rather than trying to justify our behavior. It is easy to fall into the trap of thinking that because we can't live up to a truth we should deny it or, worse, attack it. Where are you allowing lies to take root in your life? When we resist truth we resist God and we resist happiness. We cannot be happy separated from the truth; we cannot be happy in a world of lies.

november 10

_____

NOISE IS THE mouthpiece of the world. Silence is the mouthpiece of God . . .

We live in a noisy world. People wake up to clock radios, listen to the news while they shower, watch television while they eat breakfast, get into the car and listen to the morning shows on the way to work, listen to music all day over the intercom, talk incessantly on the phone between any number of meetings . . . We need a break from the noise.

Everything great in history has arisen from silence . . . even great noise. Beethoven and Mozart closed themselves off from the world and inhabited silent rooms for days at a time in order to hear things that no one else could hear—sounds so glorious that they themselves would never hear in the midst of the world, and yet sounds that the world would never know if Beethoven and Mozart had not befriended silence . . .

Why do we fear and avoid silence? The truth is, most people believe that everything within them is worthless and embarrassing. That is why we live in a world terrified of silence and full of people dedicated to imitating other people instead of developing the unique individual that they are themselves.

november 11

———————

MAXIMILIAN KOLBE was a priest in Poland during World War II. After Germany invaded Poland he organized a temporary hospital in the monastery where he lived, with the help of a few brothers who remained. Between 1939 and 1941 they provided shelter and care for thousands of refugees who were fleeing Nazi persecution.

Kolbe was arrested by the Gestapo and sent to Auschwitz. In July 1941 a man escaped from the camp. The deputy commander picked ten men to be starved to death in an underground bunker to discourage others from trying to escape. One of the men selected cried out, "My wife! My children!" Kolbe volunteered to take his place.

We hear the story of Maximilian Kolbe and it was awe-inspiring. Why are we so amazed? Is it because we couldn't imagine ourselves doing the same? And yet somehow we seem to forget that it is in no way original. Jesus taught Maximilian Kolbe how to take someone else's place, and he taught you and me when he took our place.

november 12

CHRISTIANITY has always been about attraction rather than promotion. As modern Christians, we need to dedicate ourselves to creating Holy Moments, to recognizing the extraordinary in the ordinary, and to living beautiful lives of simple holiness.

But this is not how we are living our lives as Christians today, and it's not how our communities are engaging with society.

We have played right into the culture's negative narrative about Christianity by settling for mediocrity spiritually and not striving to live more authentic Christian lives. As a result, we have an identity crisis…

This crisis is the natural result of us not living the Christian faith dynamically enough to convince society that what they have been told about us is lies.

The first Christians differentiated themselves from society. Modern Christians blend in.

november 13

_____

OUR LIVES are full of gifts, such as food, clothing, friends, and homes, to name only a few. Each of us has varying abilities to read and write, to sing and act, to laugh and make others laugh, to teach and to learn, to run and to swim, to play guitar or piano, to invent, to paint, to bear and raise children—the list is as long as there are people on this planet.

We are all given many gifts and talents. The secret to success and happiness lies not merely in having these gifts and talents but in recognizing where they come from. God is the giver of gifts.

When we see the things, people, and abilities in our lives as gifts from God, we live humbly in the presence of the Lord and we dance for joy. There is no such thing as a self-made man. This concept is the height of human pride and arrogance. God makes men and women; He gives us abilities and talents. He gives us air to breathe and food to eat while we set about building our empires on this earth. Then, when we have built our empires, we seem to forget who created them, who gifted them, and who continues to sustain our lives.

november 14

_____

WEARY IS A sure sign that God is not in these plans. "Come to me, all you who are weary and burdened," Jesus says, "and I will give you rest. Take my yoke upon you and learn from me, for I am gentle and humble of heart, and you will find rest for your souls. For my yoke is easy and my burden is light" (Matthew 11:28–30).

Are you weary? Tired? Burned out? Worn out? Overwhelmed? The bad fruit of busy just keeps piling up. Busy leads to overwhelmed, overwhelmed leads to weary, and weary leads to discouraged. Discouraged is another sure sign that God is far from our plans. And yet, it is also among the most common emotions in society today.

The daily habit of prayer gives us an opportunity to consider and regulate commitments before we agree to them. Sitting with God in the classroom of silence we can explore why we feel called or compelled to agree to add something to our schedule? What are our reasons and motives? Do we have a great desire to it? Do we feel called by God to do it? Or do we feel pressured by family and friends or other external forces?

november 15

THE GREAT MAJORITY of people do not have energy to do the things they love when they come home from work. Some will say it is because they work too hard. Others will say it is because they have so much work to do. But in truth, it is neither of these things. How many millions of people come home from work each night and plant themselves in front of the television for the evening? There are many passions and interests they would rather pursue than plant themselves for hours on end in front of the television each night. But they don't. Why? They don't have the energy.

Worse than that is our inability to recognize the flow of energy in our own lives. So many people look at watching television as a way to rest and relax. But when was the last time you got up from watching television with more energy than when you sat down? If the next leap in human excellence will be the result of energy management, we need to become infinitely familiar with the people, places, things, and activities that energize us—and equally familiar with the people, places, things, and activities that drain our energy.

november 16

———————————

WE LIVE IN a world of unlimited possibilities, but too often we get caught up in the day-to-day realities of life and the hustle and bustle of the world and lose sight of all that is possible. The busier our lives become, the more important it is to live with great intentionality. The more options we have before us, the more important it is to discern and decide with great intentionality. And living with great intentionality requires that we step back from time to time and think about life. We live more fulfilling lives when we pause each day to think about who we are, what we are here for, what matters most, what matters least, and our hopes and dreams for tomorrow.

november 17

OVER TIME the daily habit of prayer helps us to develop a deep unwavering peace about who we are, where we are, and what we are doing. It helps us to realize how few things really matter in the grand scheme of things—and there is actually a grand scheme of things.

Prayer is the antidote for the poison of busyness. It is by establishing a habit of daily prayer that we get clear about what matters most and what matters least. It helps us to gradually discover who we are and the meaning and purpose of our lives. Prayer inspires us to live with great intention and avoid wasting our lives. Busy drags our lives out of focus. Prayer brings our lives into focus.

You are where you are right now for a reason. So let me ask you, have you ever really tried prayer as a central component of your life? Sure, we have all dabbled in it from time to time. But have you ever given it a real place in your life? If you have, great. Are you willing to take it to the next level? If you haven't, are you willing to try placing prayer at the center of your days? Either way, you have a decision to make. Choose carefully. It is one of the biggest decisions you will ever make.

november 18

GOD IS YOUR FATHER. He is a loving Father with wonderful plans for His children. Regardless of the greatest plan you can put together for yourself with the greatest power of your imagination, His plan is better, greater, more exciting, and more rewarding. Believe in His plan. Ask Him to reveal His plan to you. Then listen . . .

november 19

IF YOU CAN TELL me what your habits are, I can tell you what sort of person you are. Socrates, Aristotle, Thomas Aquinas, and Ignatius of Loyola established that habits create character. Good habits create good character, and bad habits create poor character. From a person's habits it is easy to deduce what his or her future will be like. The good character created by good habits in turn creates a prosperous future. The bad character created by bad habits in turn creates misery in your future.

The good news is we can change our habits. What new habits are you trying to form in your life right now? If you can tell me, I can tell you how your future will be different from your past, because our lives change when our habits change. Most people live in the misguided fantasy that one day they will wake up and suddenly their lives will be magically different. Others live in the illusion that if they make more money, get a new car, buy a bigger house, get a promotion, or vacation in the Bahamas, then their lives will change. This doesn't work either. Our lives change when our habits change.

november 20

WHEN WE LOOK forward in our lives we see uncertainty. When we look back, the events of our lives fall
together like the colored pieces in a kaleidoscope, forming
a pattern with meaning. We are then able to see how certain circumstances and events of the past have been part
of an unfolding plan. By recognizing that a plan or pattern
of providence has been at work in our past, we are able to
move forward with trust despite the uncertainty that lies
ahead.

november 21

I GREW UP in Australia and I was twenty-two years old before I experienced my first American Thanksgiving, with a large family in Medford Lakes, New Jersey. When it came time for each person around the table to say what he or she was grateful for, my eyes began to fill with tears. To hear each person express gratitude, from infant children who were just learning to speak, to grown men and women experiencing the pressures of daily life, was awe-inspiring.

Giving thanks warms the soul and reminds us that life is an extraordinary privilege. Joy doesn't come from having, but from appreciating what we have. You can possess all the treasures, pleasures, and blessings this world has to offer, but if you don't appreciate them they will never bring you any real satisfaction.

Joy is the fruit of appreciation.

november 22

THE PURPOSE OF prayer is to help you make the journey ... to become the-best-version-of-yourself, which indeed is the purpose of life. The common mistake is to think of prayer as easy. I assure you, prayer is the most difficult thing in the world to do ... In prayer we come face-to-face with ourselves and face-to-face with God, and at different times both of these encounters can be very frightening. Prayer is difficult. But those who learn to master prayer come to master themselves, and those who come to master themselves become the instruments of tremendous good and are able to master every other human activity.

_____

ONCE UPON A TIME there was a prince. The prince was a fine young man, caring in every way, but he had a hunchback. One day the people of the area decided to build a statue in honor of the prince. The statue, however, stood straight and tall with no hunchback. Every day the prince would walk to the center of town and would stand there for a short time looking at the statue. As time passed, the people began to notice that the hunch in the prince's back was not so bad—until finally one day the prince stood straight and tall with no hunchback at all.

Read the life of Christ. Meditate on the different passages. Imagine yourself present in the different scenes. Rediscover the gospels. Prayer brings to our lives focus and direction and protects us from disordered attachments. Prayer confirms our hearts, minds, wills, and intellects in what we really want. One of the greatest problems in the world is that people do not really know what they want. Prayer allows us to clarify why we are here on this earth and reminds us that there is more to our lives than the time we spend here.

Prayer puts us in touch with eternal realities.

november 24

_____

I GOT SAD, started second-guessing myself about just about everything, felt betrayed and began feeling down, fell into the trap of becoming overly focused on myself, felt discouraged, and just generally was a bit lost. I don't know how he picks his moments, but at just the right time I felt God's hand on my shoulder, encouraging me to wake up, look around, get grateful, focus on the basics, and start living again.

Life is for living, and the best living is done amid the ordinary things of each day. The modern culture's disdain for the ordinary and worship of the extraordinary has rendered us oblivious to the amazing things in front of us, around us, and within us right now.

There is a lesson there for me, and perhaps for you too. Every time I make a conscious effort to simplify my life, I become a-better-version-of-myself, I breathe easier and deeper, and life is better. But the world is constantly trying to heap complexity upon me, and I allow it to. I let this happen. I am no victim. My life is my own, to live and to answer for.

november 25

IN OUR LIVES, we often wait too long to reflect and celebrate, or simply reflect on things too seldom. Parenting is not some- thing we should reflect upon and celebrate only at graduations and weddings. It is something we should reflect upon and celebrate often, perhaps every day. Parenting is not about one great success—graduation, marriage, a successful career, wealth, fame, status. No, parenting is about everyday success. At the end of each day we should be able to look at the parenting stoplight and think: Green, yellow, or red? This simple self-assessment allows us to gauge how we are doing as parents. If you assess yourself as a red today, you know why, and chances are you know what to do about it. If you assess yourself as yellow today, the same is probably true. If you assess yourself as green, you know tomorrow is a new day and it is likely going to take all the patience and self-possession you can muster to do it again. Success as a parent doesn't come in one fell swoop. Parenting success is one day at a time.

november 26

EVERYWHERE WE TURN there is generosity. The daily generosity of parents and the sacrifices they make for their children; the incredible generosity of our priests, men who give their lives to serve God's people and lead them spiritually; the courageous generosity of all those who serve in the military; and humanity's constant efforts to relieve the suffering of the poor and the marginalized. And still, it is so easy for us to selfishly focus on ourselves. But with every passing day, God is gently inviting us to live more generously, calling us to switch the focus off ourselves and onto others.

"It is better to give than to receive." (Acts 20:35) The more we are mindful of how much we have received, the more we are inclined to look for opportunities to give. God is the supreme giver, and whenever we give we grow in the image of God, become a-better-version-of-ourselves, and live holy lives.

When we are at our best as human beings, we are filled with an eagerness to do good, an eagerness to give generously, and an eagerness to help our brothers and sisters regardless of what ocean or idea separates us.

november 27

THE INTERESTING THING is that God wants you to have complete joy. He created you for it. Jesus came so that you could be immersed in complete joy: "I have told you this so that my joy might be in you and your joy might be complete" (John 15:11).

Is your joy complete? If it isn't, why? What is diminishing your joy? Who or what is robbing you of joy? What's standing in the way of the complete joy that Jesus wants for you? How hard are you willing to work for that joy? What are you willing to sacrifice in order to have that complete joy? Are you getting in the way of your own joy?

And, perhaps the question in all of this: Does the Gospel offer the best path to this complete joy?

Start to embrace the Gospel more—a little more, a lot more; that's up to you. But start to intentionally live the Gospel more each day. As you do, pay attention to the joy that increases in you. Pay attention to the clarity you have about what really matters and what doesn't. Pay attention to the stress and anxiety as it diminishes. Pay attention.

november 28

_____

THE PRESENT MOMENT can be brutal, and God can seem very far away . . .

I was sad and disillusioned; I felt like my compass was broken. How had I gotten it so wrong? When you think you know the will of God and you surrender yourself to it, and then something prevents you from pursuing that path, you begin to doubt your ability to discern what God is calling you to, even in the smallest things.

Almost thirty years later I understand that God was at work in that moment of rejection, but it still hurts, even today. In that moment it was impossible for my young and inexperienced self to realize that God is constantly at work—that when men block God's way, he finds another way. Today, I can look back and see that God had not abandoned me; his hand was on my shoulder, guiding me and protecting me, and he had dreams for me that I could not even imagine. We see what is possible based on what has been done in the past, but God sees new possibilities.

november 29

IF THERE IS ONE battle that resistance has dominated in the hearts and minds of Catholics for the past fifty years, it surrounds confession. We just stopped going. On one level it makes complete sense. When you stop striving for excellence, you stop yearning for coaching. Mediocrity seeks comfort and going to confession isn't comfortable. It's uncomfortable to look at ourselves, assess our selfishness and sinfulness, and tell another human being about it. But wow, is it good for us. We all have a great need for healing. We all need to be liberated from our self-centeredness. We need to grow in awareness of how what we do and say affects the people around us and people on the other side of the world. But we resist it. We resist God. We resist his forgiveness. We resist happiness.

november 30

———————

IT IS A STRANGE thing, but I have noticed that even a blind man knows when he is in the presence of a great light. The world needs you to be such a light.

december

december 1

_____

IN THE SILENCE, we see at one time the person we are now and the person we are capable of becoming. In seeing these two visions at one time, we are automatically challenged to change and grow and become the-best-version-of-ourselves. It is precisely for this reason that we fill our lives with noise, to distract ourselves from the challenge to change . . .

Writing about the importance of silence and solitude, Blaise Pascal, the seventeenth-century French philosopher, scientist, mathematician, and writer, wrote: "All of man's miseries derive from not being able to sit quietly in a room alone."

december 2

———————

I BEGIN MY PRAYER by affirming my belief that Jesus is present and that He sees and hears me. Then I continue to speak to Him in a mental conversation just as I would speak to a good friend. I tell Him about my worries, and He seems to lift the weight from my heart. I tell Him about my plans, my dreams, my friends, my family, my travels, and anything that is weighing on my heart or mind. I ask Him to point out to me my mistakes and faults. Most important, I speak to Him about decisions I need to make.

Toward the end of my prayer time I try to make one resolution for that day. I ask Jesus for the strength and grace to live that resolution. Then at night before I go to bed I examine myself in the area of the resolution I made.

I try to continue this conversation with Jesus throughout the day. I invite Him to join me in my various activities. Prayer is about living in the presence of God. It doesn't have to be something that is confined to a few moments each day. By recognizing that "God is with us" before we begin each task, our lives become one continuous road to Emmaus.

december 3

THE SAINTS are such good friends. They encourage us to love God and neighbor more fully and challenge us to use the daily events of our lives to become a-better-version-of-ourselves. But the real beauty is found in their method: They don't preach endless sermons, and they don't try to impose their views on others—they challenge, inspire, and encourage us simply by living their own lives to the fullest. That is the social dynamic of holiness. It is attractive and it is contagious. If you and I sit down at lunch and you order soup and a salad, it makes me think twice about ordering a double bacon cheeseburger and fries. If my friends are going to the gym after work, I feel that inner nudge to work out myself. If a colleague is honest and humble about a mistake he has made, I am humbled by his example. Goodness is contagious. The problem is, so is evil. The challenge for you and me, as Christians in the midst of the modern world, is to be examples of good living.

december 4

YOU SIMPLY never can get enough of what you don't really need. What is it that we really need? We don't need more money, faster cars, bigger houses, or grander promotions. The human person needs one thing above all else: intimacy. We continue to chase our illegitimate wants and neglect our legitimate needs. The result is that we live in restless discontent. Contentment is to be found only by creating a lifestyle that tends to our legitimate needs, physical, emotional, intellectual, and spiritual. Intimacy is one of our real and legitimate needs, and all the pleasures, possessions, and achievements on the planet will not satisfy you as the fulfillment of your legitimate needs will. The mutual fulfilling of legitimate needs is the pinnacle of relationships. This is what it means to be soul mates. Do you ever get the feeling that something is wrong, or that something is missing in your life? Do you ever get the sense that there must be more to life?

Something is wrong.

Something is missing.

There is more.

december 5

RELATIONSHIPS keep us honest. They provide the mirrors necessary to see and know ourselves. Isolated and alone, we can convince ourselves of all sorts of crazy things, but other people keep it real for us by drawing us out of our own imaginary worlds.

They don't allow us to deceive ourselves. Other people keep us honest. Relationships help to move us out of our illusions and into reality

december 6

THE ONLY WAY to say no to anything is to have a deeper yes.

december 7

_____

IN MY OWN journey, there is one question that towers above all others. In fact, in many ways this one question has defined my journey. It is this: God, what do you think I should do? I ask it when small decisions lay before me. I ask it in my time for prayer and reflection each day about the larger questions that loom before me.

You are making decisions every single day of your life—as a person, as a spouse, as a parent, as an employee, and as a citizen. Some of them are small and some of them could alter the whole direction of your life and relationships. When was the last time you sat down in the classroom of silence with the Divine Architect and said, "Show me the plan." When was the last time you sat down with the Divine Navigator and said, "Give me some direction." When was the last time you stepped into the classroom of silence, and sat with your God, and said, "God, what do you think I should do?" This is the question that should dominate your inner dialogue.

december 8

————————

MY LIFE has been remarkably blessed. I suspect I have experienced more joy than most, and while there have certainly been dark moments in my journey, I have not suffered anywhere near as much as some. But I do witness human suffering in all its forms. Sometimes it is the result of an accident, and at other times it is the aftermath of a natural disaster. However, it seems to me that the great majority of suffering people experience in this world is because we don't live up to the great human commission. The commission consists simply of being human. It is when we are less than human that we bring suffering upon others. Animals are not capable of patience, compassion, generosity, or any of the greatness that tis uniquely human.

Religion is the primary humanizing force in a person, in a society, in history. In my own experience this is particularly true of the Catholic form of Christianity. Catholicism makes me a–better-version-of-myself. It makes me more human.

december 9

GOD NEVER GOES BACK; he always moves forward. Adam and Eve were banished from the garden. God could have redeemed them and sent them back to the garden, but he didn't, for two reasons: God always wants our future to be bigger than our past, and God always moves forward.

december 10

_____

LOVE IS A CHOICE, and an important one, because we become what we love. What we love intrigues our hearts and captures our imagination. We spend our days thinking about what we love. Thought determines action, actions determine habits, habits determine character, and your character is your destiny.

What are you in love with? What fascinates you? What intrigues you and captures your imagination? Nothing will affect your life more than whom and what you choose to love. Pedro Arrupe explained it in this way. "What you are in love with, what seizes your imagination, will affect everything. It will decide what will get you out of bed in the morning, what you do with your evenings, how you spend your weekends, what you read, who you know, what breaks your heart, and what amazes you with joy and gratitude. Fall in love, stay in love, and it will decide everything."

HOLINESS IS possible for you! You can collaborate with God to create Holy Moments. Try it today. In the process you will become a-better-version-of-yourself, help others become a-better-version-of-themselves, and make the world a better place. Don't waste another moment—remind yourself over and over again that it is possible. Modern culture says holiness is not possible. It's a lie. If you can create one Holy Moment, that proves holiness is possible for you. Modern culture has robbed billions of people of happiness by discouraging them in their Christianity and convincing them of this single lie that holiness is not possible. But today is a day of liberation. Today I hope you have been liberated from that lie and as a result the whole world looks different.

Holiness is possible for you. This beautiful truth is the opposite of the diabolical neutralizing lie that has paralyzed so many Christians and their communities. It should be no surprise that one of the greatest truths in the history of Christianity is the exact opposite of the biggest lie in the history of Christianity. Holiness is possible, one moment at a time. This single beautiful truth can change your life forever, beginning today, beginning right now.

december 12

I WALKED into a bookstore recently and sitting on the shelves in the front of the store were several large coffee-table books. One in particular caught my eye, so I walked over to have a look. For the next ten minutes, I flipped through the pages of two books, glancing at the pictures, and a great fire was fanned in my heart. One was about the life of Mother Teresa and the other about the life of John Paul II. The world has a great need for the example of authentic lives because we all need to be inspired. We need to be reminded of what is possible. These people have allowed God to fill them with his love, and the glow of that love alive in them is blinding. The power of their lives and the greatness of their spirits cannot be adequately put into words. But occasionally, in the memory of an event in their lives, or in the story a photo tells, we catch a glimpse. Just passing through those pages, glancing at the pictures, elevated my heart and made my spirit soar. Just looking at those pictures made me want to be a better person—I didn't even read a word. That is the power of these great lives.

december 13

I CHALLENGE YOU to ask yourself this question today and every day. What is my relationship with Jesus like today? Is it a friendship? Does it need work? Do you need to make amends? Is it consistent? Do you only come to Jesus when you want something?

Jesus is your friend; He has all the answers and desires a personal relationship with you. Sometimes friendship means talking, and sometimes it means listening. It is wisdom to know the difference. Prayer is not about all sorts of fancy petitions and sayings. Prayer is not a psychological mind game. It is an action of love that takes place between the spirit within you and the Spirit of God.

Sometimes when we are with a friend, it is not necessary for either person to speak. It is comforting, refreshing, and renewing just to be with that person. And so it is in our relationship with God.

december 14

_____

OFFER THE LEAST enjoyable tasks of your day to God as a prayer for someone who is suffering.

december 15

THE AUTHENTIC LIFE begins with the simple desire to be who God created us to be and cooperate with God by playing the part he has designed for us in human history. The adventure of salvation begins when we stop asking, "What's in it for me?" and turn humbly to God in our hearts and ask, How may I serve? What work do you wish for me to do with my life? What is your will for my life?

God calls each of us to live an authentic life. He has designed this life to perfectly integrate our legitimate needs, our deepest desires, and our unique talents. The more intimately and harmoniously these three are related, the more you become truly yourself.

december 16

_____

ONCE WHEN I was speaking in Canada, I asked my audience this question, "If I put a hundred million dollars on the ground in front of you and told you if you come back tomorrow you can each take a thousand dollars, who wouldn't come back?"One humorous man in the audience exclaimed, "I wouldn't go home." Again we all laughed.

Supposing I put that money in your church and told you that if you went to visit your local church tomorrow and spent ten minutes in prayer you could take ten thousand dollars. Would you make it to your church tomorrow if you knew ten thousand dollars were waiting for you?

Most of us are busy people with a lot of things to do. But for ten thousand dollars we'd make time, we would give it top priority—but visiting Jesus, who is our greatest friend, who has all the answers, and who will set our minds at ease, is not important enough to go out of our way. Has money become our God? For how long will we continue to neglect prayer?

december 17

LIFE IS PRIORITY driven.

Whatever you place your attention on will increase in your life. If you are constantly thinking and talking about everything you are grateful for in your life, the number of things you have to be grateful for will increase. If you are constantly preoccupied with all the things you don't have, the number of things you wish you had will increase. Human thought is creative. What we think becomes. Everything begins first as a thought in our minds.

If we are serious about giving priority to our relationship, we must first give it priority in our minds. Before all else, you must know what a great relationship looks like to you. You must begin by clearly identifying the qualities necessary to build and sustain extraordinary relationships.

december 18

I LOVE BEING around people who are striving to love God and better themselves. They energize me. They inspire me. They challenge me. They make me want to be a better person. This is true friendship. A true friend brings the best out of his or her friends. You cannot convince me that someone who is not helping you to become the-best-version-of-yourself is a good friend. For this reason, when I have time to spend with friends, I try to surround myself with people who make me want to be a better person. I admit they are not easy to find, but when you do find them, they are more precious than any treasure or pleasure this world has to offer. If you want a litmus test for choosing friends, use this question: Will spending time with this person make me a better person?

december 19

—————————

ALL OF LIFE'S important relationships thrive under
the condition of carefree timelessness. Learn to waste time
with the people you love.

december 20

OUR WORLD IS changing so quickly. It can be a little frightening at times. It is easy to become so busy worrying about the future that we forget to live our dreams. There is something wonderful about a dream. It is not the achievement of the dream that matters most, but rather the pursuit of those dreams that are born from deep within us. The pursuit of the dream is life; it does something mysterious to us, fills us with hope, passion, and enthusiasm, and expands our capacities as a human person in every way.

So what are we waiting for? We get only one shot at life. Isn't it time for a little soul-searching? Visit a quiet church in the middle of the day. Take a walk in the park. Turn off the television and talk to your children. Open the paper and look for the job you've always wanted. Keep a promise. Tell your mum you love her. Restore an old Ford. Make friends with your neighbors. Say yes instead of maybe. Watch a sunset. Write your spouse a love letter. Fly a kite. Say sorry. Ask that girl out on a date. Try a food you've never tasted before. Make peace with God.

december 21

HERE ON MY DESK in my study where I write, I have an hourglass. I turn it on its head, and it empties the sand out in a perfect hour. You may wonder why it is such a powerful tool for me. The reason is that in a sense, time is always being lost. You never find time. Time is either used wisely or wasted foolishly. We wear watches and look at clocks. Their hands go around and around or they have digital numbers that renew themselves with the same frequency. All of this creates the illusion that time is constantly there. It gives the impression that time is circular. It is not. Time is linear. Once it has passed, it has passed.

There is power in this moment. Use it, direct it, harness it. Moments are like the petals of a rose; they fall to the ground if there is no life in them.

december 22

WHO ARE YOU? In many different ways, people try to discover who they truly are as individuals. Some go off into the mountains, some travel to distant lands, others go to monasteries and convents, some walk up and down the beach early each morning, and still others seek to discover themselves through writing or music . . .

You may try any path you wish. You may try to find yourself in a thousand different ways, but in a wonderfully profound and mysterious way, it is only through self-donation—giving ourselves to others—that we discover our true self.

december 23

_____

WHOM DOES YOUR LIFE intrigue? Not with spectacular accomplishments, but simply by the way you live, love, and work.

If we live and love the way the Gospel invites us to, we will intrigue people. Respect and cherish your spouse and children, and people will be intrigued. Work hard and pay attention to the details of your work, and you will intrigue people. Go out of your way to help those in need, people will be intrigued. When we do what is right even if it comes at a great cost to ourselves, people are intrigued. Patience, kindness, humility, gratitude, thoughtfulness, generosity, courage and forgiveness are all intriguing.

december 24

LIFE'S NOT ABOUT money. Life is not about what sort of position or what sort of power you have. It's not about whether you're famous. It's not about whether or not you vacation in all the right places every year. Life's not about what sort of clothes you wear and whether they have fancy labels that massively increase their price. Life is not about these things.

Life's not about who you've dated or who you're dating. Life's not about who your parents are or whom you know. Life's not even about what sort of grades you get in school; your parents and your teachers don't want me to tell you that, but it's true. Life is not about these things.

Life is about love. It's about whom you love and whom you hurt. Life's about how you love yourself and how you hurt yourself. Life's about how you love and hurt the people close to you. Life is about how you love and hurt the people who just cross your path for a moment.

Life is about love.

december 25

PLANNING IS good and necessary up to a point, but we find God in the now. God lives in the eternal now. He is constantly inviting us to immerse ourselves in the present moment so we can be with him.

Sometimes planning the future can be a way of avoiding the present, and when we avoid the present we avoid God. Sometimes having everything in its place can be a way of trying to be in control, and sometimes it is a way of distracting ourselves from what really matters right now. Often we find God in the mess of our lives, the mess of our personalities, and the mess of our own brokenness.

One of the greatest mistakes in history has been to go off looking for God in the extraordinary. God occasionally uses the extraordinary to get our attention, but since the beginning his favorite place has been amid the very ordinary things of life. A child in a manger—what could be more ordinary?

december 26

SOONER OR LATER we realize that what the world has to offer is simply not enough to satisfy us. It is only then that most of us turn to four of life's biggest questions:

- Who am I?
- What am I here for?
- What matters most?
- What matters least?

Our curiosity about these important questions reveals our zest for life. In each of these questions is an acknowledgment that we are each unique, that life has meaning and purpose, that life is short, and that we are pilgrims passing through this world, grasping at happiness and curious to know the answers to these questions and so much more. For many people curiosity peaks between the ages of two and three, partially as a result of being told to stop asking why. It's time to reignite your curiosity about who you are, what you are here for, what matters most, and what matters least, so that you can start living…

december 27

LIFE PASSES US by so quickly. Think of it like this: let's assume that you will live for seventy-five years. Now suppose that you have just the next five minutes in which to decide what you want to do for the rest of your life. Your life, compared to eternity, is like those five minutes, and in this life, you must decide what you want to do for eternity. Five minutes compared to seventy-five years is almost insignificant. Seventy-five years compared to eternity holds even less significance.

There is another world, and all of us one day will find ourselves in it. The decisions and actions of our lives will determine where we take up lodging in the next world. There is joy and there is misery. No one can force either upon you. It is the exercise of your free will that will determine which you experience now and in eternity. The very foundation of this life is prayer and growth in virtue. It is only by embracing these that our true selves emerge.

december 28

"IF YOU ARE what you should be you will set the world ablaze." These words were famously penned in the fourteenth century by Catherine of Siena. It's an arresting idea for a number of reasons. We all have a sense of who we are capable of being, and a sense that we are not quite living up to our potential. But the quote also rightly points out that there are natural consequences for the whole world when we find and live out our mission in life. When we are faithful to who God created us to be, and what God calls us to do, incredible things happen.

december 29

_____

NOW IT IS YOUR TURN. Identify some core habits for yourself. Start with one. I began with one many years ago. It has taken me more than a decade to build up to five daily core habits. How do you get started? Ask yourself, "What would be a game changer for my days? What one thing, if done every day, would change my life markedly?"

Once you identify your first core habit, measure it. How many days a week do you do it? Perhaps it is four or five times the first week. Very well, beat that the next week. How many days do you do it the first month? Whatever the number, accept it as a challenge to do better the next month. But measuring it is critical. You will be amazed how hard it is to implement one life-changing daily habit . . .

Once you are able to follow this habit about 80 percent of the time, add another core habit. Keep following the process until you get to the four or five things that ensure you have a really good day. Every year is made up of three hundred and

december 30

THE SAINTS were remarkable men and women, but surprisingly what made them remarkable was rarely anything too spectacular. What made them extraordinary was the ordinary. They strove to grow in virtue through the ordinary things of everyday life.

There is something ultimately attractive about holiness. When holiness emerges in any place and time, all men and women of good will are inspired. What is it that makes them so attractive? Perhaps it is their humble surrender to the will of God and the joy that emerges from that surrender. Perhaps it is the many virtues that they acquire along the way: patience, kindness, humility, gentleness, forgiveness, and love. Or is it their desire to explore their God-given potential? This quality is incredibly attractive and ultimately inspiring. Or perhaps it is that they are not proud and arrogant about who they are and what they have done. Or maybe it's just that they are focused on loving God and neighbor by becoming the-best-version-of-themselves.

LORD, HERE I AM.

I trust that you have an incredible plan for me.

Transform me. Transform my life.

Everything is on the table.

Take what you want to take and give what you want to give. I make myself 100 percent available to you today. Transform me into the person you created me to be, so I can live the life you envisioned for me at the beginning of time.

I hold nothing back.

I am 100 percent available.

Lead me, challenge me, encourage me, and open my eyes to all your possibilities.

Show me what it is you want me to do, and I will do it.

Amen.

If you want to see miracles, pray that prayer. If you want to see and experience miracles in your own life, pray a wholehearted prayer of transformation. That's a prayer God will answer.

Matthew Kelly was born in Sydney, Australia. He has dedicated his life to helping people and organizations become the-best-version-of-themselves. Kelly is a New York Times bestselling author, an internationally acclaimed speaker, and a business consultant to some of the world's largest and most admired companies. He is the author of more than twenty books, which have sold more than forty million copies and have been published in more than thirty languages.

www.MatthewKelly.com